Wikis: Tools for Information Work and Collaboration

CHANDOS
INFORMATION PROFESSIONAL SERIES

Series Editor: Ruth Rikowski
(email: Rikowskigr@aol.com)

Chandos' new series of books are aimed at the busy information professional. They have been specially commissioned to provide the reader with an authoritative view of current thinking. They are designed to provide easy-to-read and (most importantly) practical coverage of topics that are of interest to librarians and other information professionals. If you would like a full listing of current and forthcoming titles, please visit our web site **www.chandospublishing.com** or contact Hannah Grace-Williams on email info@chandospublishing.com or telephone number +44 (0) 1865 884447.

New authors: we are always pleased to receive ideas for new titles; if you would like to write a book for Chandos, please contact Dr Glyn Jones on email gjones@chandospublishing.com or telephone number +44 (0) 1865 884447.

Bulk orders: some organisations buy a number of copies of our books. If you are interested in doing this, we would be pleased to discuss a discount. Please contact Hannah Grace-Williams on email info@chandospublishing.com or telephone number +44 (0) 1865 884447.

Wikis: Tools for Information Work and Collaboration

JANE KLOBAS

WITH ADDITIONAL CONTRIBUTIONS FROM
ANGELA BEESLEY
KRISTÍN Ó HLYNSDÓTTIR
MARCO MARLIA
PRU MITCHELL
AND
SÉBASTIEN PAQUET

Chandos Publishing
Oxford · England

Chandos Publishing (Oxford) Limited
Chandos House
5 & 6 Steadys Lane
Stanton Harcourt
Oxford OX29 5RL
UK
Tel: +44 (0) 1865 884447 Fax: +44 (0) 1865 884448
Email: info@chandospublishing.com
www.chandospublishing.com

First published in Great Britain in 2006

ISBN:
1 84334 178 6 (paperback)
1 84334 179 4 (hardback)
978 1 84334 178 9 (paperback)
978 1 84334 179 6 (hardback)

© J. Klobas, 2006

Typeset by Domex e-Data Pvt. Ltd.
Printed in the UK and USA.

To Laurel Anne Clyde

Contents

List of figures and tables

Figures

Tables

Preface

[The World Wide Web would be] an information space through which people can communicate, but communicate in a special way: communicate by sharing their knowledge in a pool. The idea was not just that it should be a big browsing medium. The idea was that everybody would be putting their ideas in, as well as taking them out. (Tim Berners-Lee, 1999)[1]

The years 2004 and 2005 were marked by a noticeable change in the Internet. Although they had been seen earlier, the number of World Wide Web-based services that enabled people not just to read what was on the Web, but also to write to the Web, reached a critical mass, and new terms were coined to describe this new phenomenon. Perhaps the most evocative of these terms is Web 2.0, coined by Tim O'Reilly and colleagues[2] to convey the sense that the Web has reached a new stage of maturity. Critical to this new maturity is participation of users in building 'collective intelligence'. Social links among users, created by the users or by software that links them based on shared interests, are as important to this more mature Web as information seeking and information provision. Instead of just being a platform for reading, or listening to or viewing broadcasts, the Web is being transformed into a 'conversational' platform. This is as much a social transformation as a technological one.

Associated with recognition of the new maturity of the Web was acknowledgement of the value of the 'long tail' of the Internet.[3] Internet resources appear to follow Pareto's Law (the 80:20 rule): while about 20 per cent of Internet resources might be valuable for 80 per cent of users, about 80 per cent of the resources might be relevant to only 20 per cent of users. Thus, an Internet resource does not have to be big or used by a large number of people to be valuable. Indeed, much of the Internet – the so-called 'long tail' – is devoted to uses by many small groups of people, for information sharing or for collaboration.

Wikis are mentioned in these discussions as enablers of collaboration across the Internet, both on a large scale – as in the wiki-based encyclopaedia, Wikipedia[4] – and in the long tail of small communities that share information and collaborate on projects in very specific fields of interest. Wikis are being widely, but quietly, used in business, and the technology is still maturing, in response to the many uses to which wikis are being put.[5]

This is the environment in which this book, written primarily for non-technical readers, was conceived. What does the book contain? Chapter 1 introduces, defines and describes wikis, emphasising their role as social information spaces. Chapter 2 examines wikis as information resources, considering the qualities of wikis as sources of information and providing a number of examples. What if you need to find a wiki? Chapter 3 reviews the available tools.

In Chapters 4 to 6, we examine how wikis are used in different fields. Chapter 4 considers how wikis are used in library and information science, one of the first disciplines outside wikis' primarily technical roots to adopt wikis for a wide range of uses. Chapter 5 presents on overview of the uses to which wikis are being put in business. In Chapter 6, the role of wikis in education is described, along with several examples.

Chapters 7 and 8 address issues associated with creating and managing wikis. Chapter 7 describes six different paths that can be taken to create a wiki and reviews some of the most well-known wiki software and hosting services. Chapter 8 examines management of wikis throughout their entire lifecycle, from planning through to evaluation, with an emphasis on practical advice for people who are planning or managing wikis.

The end product is a book written for people who want to find out about wikis and their potential; for readers who want to know more about wikis as social information spaces and information resources, and wikis in library and information science, business and education; for people who do not necessarily have a technical background but want to create a wiki; and for those who are planning or trying to a manage a wiki. While this is not a technical book, readers with a technical background should find it technically accurate and, we hope, interesting. For readers, new and old to wikis, we hope this book expands your understanding of what it means to collaborate and how wikis can be used to support collaboration and provide information.

While 2005 was an important year for the Web, it also saw the death of Anne Clyde (who often wrote as Laurel A. Clyde), a pioneer in the study of the Internet and its role in learning. Anne's death in September was a shock to her many friends and colleagues around the world. She had several projects in progress. One of them was a book about wikis. She had developed an outline, entered into an agreement with Chandos Publishing, and begun research for the book, but had not yet begun to write. With the support of Glyn Jones of Chandos, the team of authors who contributed to this book completed it to Anne's initial outline. We dedicate this book to Anne Clyde.

The contributors to this book represent a wide range of people who work with wikis. Angela Beesley is a member of the Board of Trustees of the Wikimedia Foundation, the body that oversees Wikipedia and other publicly available wiki reference works. Angela is also the founder and manager of the Wikia wiki hosting service and well qualified to contemplate the issues associated with managing wikis (Chapter 8). Kristin Hlynsdóttir (Chapter 4, Wikis in library and information science) is a web manager and records manager at the Icelandic Land Registry and teaches information retrieval – including use of wikis as information resources – to students of library and information science at the University of Iceland. Jane Klobas is a business school academic with an interest in uses of the Internet in education and information work. Jane uses wikis for collaboration in teaching and research. While completing his business degree and a thesis on online communities, groupware and e-learning, Marco Marlia (Chapter 7, Creating a wiki – the technology choices) co-founded two companies involved in web design, hosting and marketing. Marco is a passionate supporter of open source initiatives, including open source wikis. Pru Mitchell, from education.au, applies her experience in evaluation of new resources for education to her review of wikis in education in Chapter 6. Seb Paquet (Chapter 5, Wikis in business) completed what was perhaps the first doctoral thesis that studied wikis. He has experience in research on innovative uses of social software and now, among other things, contributes to thinking at Socialtext, Inc., one of the first commercial providers of wiki software.

Many other people contributed information for this book. Particular thanks go to Guy Fraser with whom I had some very enjoyable and valuable e-mail conversations about wikis as I struggled with some of the more difficult and obscure issues in preparing this book, and to Gerry McKiernan of Iowa State University who posted a request for information on my behalf to 14 lists. Thanks to all who responded to requests for information, including Karen Anderson, Randal Baier, Stefano Basaglia, Charles Blair, Vincent Briggeman, Stacy Chaney, Jon Haupt, John Hubbard, Robert Jackson, Brian Kelly, Ann Majchrzak,

Susan Maret, Brad Matthies, David Mattison, Ross Mayfield, Benjamin Naftzger, David Petersen, Larry Press, Lauren Pressley, Mark Roseman, Todd Quinn, David Rosen, Hans Scheibler, Karen Schneider, and Beverly Trayner, Sharon Wightman, Ösp Viggósdóttir. Thanks, too, to all involved in the production of this book: the authors, Angela Beesley, Kristin Hlynsdóttir, Marco Marlia, Pru Mitchell, Sébastien Paquet; Stefano Renzi for administration of the JotSpot-hosted wiki that we used to support our work; and Glyn Jones for being a model publisher for the Internet era. In addition to their official roles, all members of the team contributed resources and commented on draft chapters, enriching the accuracy and readability of this book.

My thanks also go to the authors and founders of the wiki sites that have been included in the book. Most wikis are the product of anonymous authors, so we have not been able to identify and obtain the permission of all contributors to the wiki sites that we have used as illustrations. Indeed, many wikis are made available under the Creative Commons Attribution 2.5 License, which we gratefully acknowledge. Where we have been able to identify an individual responsible for a site or image, we have sought their permission. Thanks go to Lyndsay Blanton of RadioReference.com, Mark Dilley of Wiki Index, Meredith Farkas for Library Success, Guy Fraser of Adaptavist.com, Chris Klaus of the National Science Digital Library, Earle Martin of the Open Guides project, Lauren Pressley, Craig Swietlik of Argonne National Laboratory, Al Upton, EdNA, JotSpot, the Veronica Research Group, Writely, and the Wikimedia Foundation. From Wikipedia, we have reproduced screens that use photographs taken by John Howard and Adam Stacey. The Wikimedia Foundation has no objection to use of a screenshot to illustrate Wikipedia, but if you have contributed a photo or other material that you see reproduced in this book and would like credit for it, please add your name to the book's wiki.

Yes, now that the book is completed and in your hands, it has its own wiki, at *www.booki.info*. We would welcome your visit to this wiki, to comment on, correct, expand or improve on the book. If you have not tried wikis before, there is a 'sandbox' (or 'sand pit' if you prefer) where you can play.

Jane Klobas
Milan, March 2006.

Notes

1. Berners-Lee, T. (1999) 'Transcript of Tim Berners-Lee's talk to the LCS 35th Anniversary celebrations, Cambridge Massachusetts, 14 April 1999'; available at: *http://www.w3.org/1999/04/13-tbl.html* (accessed: 18 February 2006). Berners-Lee is recognised as the inventor of the World Wide Web.
2. O'Reilly, T. (2005) 'What is Web 2.0: Design patterns and business models for the next generation of software'; available at: *http://oreillynet.com/lpt/a/6228* (accessed: 3 March 2006).
3. The long tail, a statistical concept, was introduced to the Internet community by Chris Anderson, who applied it to the entertainment industry: Anderson, C. (2004) 'The long tail', *Wired Magazine* 12(10); available at: *http://www.wired.com/wired/archive/12.10/tail.html* (accessed: 2 March 2006).
4. By April 2005, Wikipedia was reported to be the second most popular reference source on the Web: Burns, E. (2005) 'Wikipedia's popularity and traffic soar', *ClickZ Network*; available at: *http://www.clickz.com/stats/sectors/traffic_patterns/article.php/3504061* (accessed: 3 March 2006).
5. Drakos, N., Linden, A., Reynolds, M. and Raskino, M. (2004) *Wikis Can Improve Collaborative Work and Knowledge Sharing*. Stamford, CT: Gartner Group; Fenn, J. and Linden, A. (2005) *Gartner's Hype Cycle Special Report for 2005*. Stamford, CT: Gartner Group.

About the contributors

Angela Beesley is a leading figure in the wiki community. Since June 2004, she has served as a member of the Board of Trustees of the Wikimedia Foundation, the non-profit organisation which runs Wikipedia, Wikibooks, Wikinews and other educational reference sites. Angela has been a volunteer editor of Wikipedia since early 2003. In 2004, she co-founded Wikia, a community-oriented wiki hosting site, with Jimmy Wales. Angela was previously a researcher and test developer for the National Foundation for Educational Research in the UK where her main role was creating the national statutory assessments for England and Wales. Prior to that, she was a researcher at the Aston Dyslexia and Developmental Assessment Centre in Birmingham, now part of the Neurosciences Research Institute. Angela has an honours degree in Human Psychology. She is currently based in Melbourne, Australia, but travels frequently.

Guy Fraser is a technophobe who loves technology. Having worked with computers and software since he first realised he hated maths, Guy has long believed that usability is the most vital aspect of any system – if it's not usable, people won't use it; if people won't use it, it's useless. He has worked with systems that allow humans to interact with each other and computers, since the age of 6, always striving for that truly useful solution. In 2005 he realised his dream and founded Adaptavist.com, a company dedicated to the use and abuse of wikis in every way imaginable. Guy is based in Cheshire, England.

Kristín Ó Hlynsdóttir is a web manager and records manager at the Icelandic Land Registry in Reykjavik, Iceland. She is also Adjunct at the Library and Information Science department at the University of Iceland. She has an MA in Information Management from the University of Brighton, UK where her main focus was on the Web and usability studies. She has been involved with web management since 1997. As a web manager she has held talks and seminars in Iceland involving corporate intranets as well as web management in libraries.

Jane Klobas is a researcher at Bocconi University in Milan, Italy, and Professorial Fellow in The Graduate School of Management at The University of Western Australia. She has a PhD in Psychology (an early study of the Internet in education), an MBA and qualifications in Library and Information Science. She has experience in information service and library management, always working with leading edge search and communication technologies. She currently teaches information systems to international MBA students in Italy and Australia, and research methods whenever and wherever she can. As a teacher and researcher, she has worked with the Internet as an information resource since the early 1990s. Her current research involves study of Internet-based collaboration in education and in international organisations. She has written widely on the Internet, its use and its impact.

Marco Marlia graduated in Economics of Financial Markets at L. Bocconi University, Milan. He has studied online communities, groupware and e-learning. He is the co-founder of Nextre Engineering S.r.l., a web software company, and Biquadra S.r.l. dedicated to Web marketing. He currently collaborates with the Institute of Quantitative Methods and the Institute for Organisation and Informative Systems at Bocconi University.

Pru Mitchell is an information officer at education.au, Australia's national ICT agency for education and training, and also a part-time reference librarian at the University of Adelaide. She has an MEd and qualifications in Library and Information Science and School Management. As a teacher librarian she has worked across the spectrum of education in K-12 schools, TAFE colleges and universities, as well as being a frequent conference presenter and contributor to the professional literature on a wide range of topics, including ICT in education libraries, professional standards, search technologies, education thesauri and metadata.

Sébastien Paquet has been involved in research and development at the intersection of social software, knowledge sharing, online communities and collaboration for the past few years. He is deeply interested in the person- and social network-centred design of information technology. He holds a BSc in Physics and a PhD in Computer Science from Université de Montreal. His doctoral dissertation examined weblogs, wikis, and ontologies as means of sharing knowledge across disciplinary boundaries. He now works for Socialtext, Inc. where he works chiefly on understanding, facilitating and documenting the use of wiki technology for collaboration. Before joining Socialtext, he was an associate research officer at the National Research Council of Canada's Institute for Information Technology, where he experimented with introducing innovative social software in educational environments. Dr Paquet serves on the committee of the International Wiki Symposium and the Social Software in the Academy Workshop, and is on the advisory board of the ELGG and Project Opus social software initiatives.

The authors may be contacted at the following:

E-mail: *wikis@unibocconi.it*

Wikis, from social software to social information space
Jane Klobas[1]

In 1999, Tim Berners-Lee described his original vision of the Web: 'people can communicate ... by sharing their knowledge in a pool ... putting their ideas in, as well as taking them out'. At the time, the Web was still primarily 'a big browsing medium' that did not live up to his vision – but wikis and other social software have changed that.

Social software

Social software is software that facilitates social interaction, collaboration and information exchange, and may even foster communities, based on the activities of groups of users.[2] In its broadest sense, social software includes any software tool that brings people together and 'supports group interaction'.[3] Tools as simple as the cc: function in e-mail can be considered social software, but the term is more often used to refer to several separate bundles of systems that evolved in the early twenty-first century. The most frequently cited of these are social classification systems,[4] blogs and wikis.[5]

Social classification systems were designed to use the linking (or, more accurately, 'hyperlinking') capabilities of the Internet to connect people on the basis of common interests.[6] With these systems, Internet users can store resources, such as photographs, on the Web and add labels (known as 'tags') to describe each stored resource. Common interests and, some say, a sense of community, can be uncovered by identifying and even contacting other people who have stored resources with the same tag. The social connections made with these systems are heavily mediated by technology.

Blogs began as journals or diaries written by individuals and published on the Web. We now see blogs written by groups and organisations. Blogs are written by typing text (and, sometimes, adding images) into an editing window in a web browser. Regular bloggers might produce an entry in this way every day. Reading a blog is like reading the entries in a diary. Blogs are regarded as social software because 'conversations' can be built on them: bloggers can link to one another's blogs using hyperlinks, and readers can comment on the content by clicking on the 'Comment' button at the end of a blog entry. Blogs, however, remain primarily a form of broadcasting where the software supports communication from one author to many readers.[7]

Wiki software permits more active social interaction. Like blogs, authors enter content using a web browser – but there are two significant differences. Wikis are thought of as tools for multiple authors rather than a single author. The authors of a wiki[8] jointly edit pages to produce a single, collaboratively authored resource. The communication model supported by wiki software is not one-to-many as with blogs, but many-to-many. Furthermore, wikis are structured by content rather than time. While blogs consist of a sequence of entries ordered by date, wikis consist of pages. Each time someone edits a wiki page, the current page is made available in its entirety to be modified. Each time a wiki is edited, the content of the resource itself changes. People not only put their ideas in; they also build on the ideas of others, sharing information and collectively developing knowledge. As we will see in this book, wikis, more than any other social software, have enabled Berners-Lee's vision to be realised, perhaps even to be surpassed.

What are wikis?

The term *wiki* is used to refer to both wiki sites and the software used to maintain them. Wiki sites are collections of interlinked documents and files accessible and editable, by web browser. They are like websites that can be developed, modified and extended by their readers (and indeed when they are open to users on the Web, they are websites, *collaboratively edited* websites). As software, wikis are collaborative authoring tools that are accessed through a web browser. Wiki software allows a pool of authors to jointly develop a wiki site. The interplay between wiki software, authors and wiki sites means that when we talk of 'a wiki', we often mean the ensemble of all these elements: the software enables people both to read and edit the content of the site, while the site that readers see has been produced by multiple authors interacting with the software to produce the resource.

The most well-known public wiki, Wikipedia, provides an excellent example of how wikis work. Wikipedia is an encyclopaedia that can be consulted online in the same way as any other encyclopaedia. But, what if you find an error? You – and 'you' means anyone – can correct it. You can change any aspect of an entry. You can, for example, correct a typographical or factual error, or add a reference or additional information. All pages have an 'Edit this page' button. Click on the button and you can edit the page, much as if you were editing a page in a word processor. Changes appear on the page immediately, in real time. For example, when the author, Umberto Eco, found two errors – a piece of biographical information and an interpretation of his work – in an otherwise accurate entry in Wikipedia, he simply corrected them using this process.[9] Furthermore, if there is no Wikipedia entry on a topic in which you have some interest or expertise, you can create it.

Figure 1.1 shows two different views of the same page taken from Wikipedia. Figure 1.1a shows the 'wiki' entry as viewed by a reader, while Figure 1.1b shows the same page as it appears to an author. The page shown in Figure 1.1a looks like – and is – a normal web page, but with an important difference: the 'Edit this page' button at the top of the entry. Clicking on the 'Edit this page' button takes you to the edit view shown in Figure 1.1b. The edit view shows the text of the entry (this looks rather formidable, but is quite easy to manipulate using the text formatting icons, and some wikis allow WYSIWYG[10] editing just like a word processor, while others display the text exactly as on the web page), some text formatting buttons and buttons that can be clicked to save, preview or cancel changes.

This example illustrates another aspect of wikis: wikis are quick (indeed, the word 'wiki' means 'quick' in Hawaiian).[11] Click on the edit button and edit the page. Make your changes, click 'save', and the changes are displayed. If you want to add a new page, just refer to it in the text as you are editing. Your saved page will show the link to your new page; just click on the link and you are editing the new page. Table 1.1 compares the wiki page editing process with the process involved in editing a standard web page: wiki page editing involves half the number of steps, each of them

Figure 1.1 (a) The Wikipedia entry for 'Wiki'; (b) the editing view of the Wikipedia entry for 'Wiki'

(a)

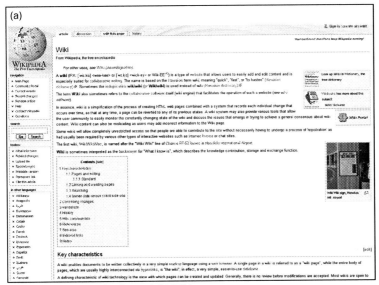

Source: *http://en.wikipedia.org/wiki/Wiki*

(b)

Source: *http://en.wikipedia.org/w/index.php?title=Wiki&action=edit*

Table 1.1 Wikis are quick: contrasting steps in editing wiki pages and web pages

Wiki page	Web page
1. Go to the page in your web browser	1. Load your web design tool (Dreamweaver, Frontpage, etc.)
2. Click edit	2. Browse to the web page on your local disk
3. Make changes	3. Open the file
4. Click save	4. Make the required changes
	5. Save the file
	6. Upload the file to your web server
	7. Open your web browser
	8. View the uploaded web page to make sure everything is ok

simpler than the steps involved in web page editing. (And that probably includes saving the file, as you will, of course, have saved the original version of your web page before you began to edit it, whereas wiki software saves the previous version automatically.)

Wikis can be available for all to read and modify on the public Web, or they can be private wikis, developed to support collaboration among a small group of known contributors. They can even be used in a hybrid form, supporting collaborative 'back-end' development of a website that can only be read by members of the public; in this case, the resource is a wiki for its authors, but an ordinary website to its readers.

What wikis are not

These features help distinguish wiki software from other forms of social software used for content publishing, communication and collaboration on the Web. We have already mentioned that wikis enable many-to-many communication, while blogs primarily support one-to-many communication; in addition, blogs are based around a timeline (the sequence of contributions by the author), while wikis focus on content (although, as we will see later, it is possible to track changes in a wiki over time). In a similar way, wikis differ from discussion forums. Instead of being based on temporal threads of a conversation that can wander from one topic to another, and where conversations on the some topic can exist in different threads, wikis structure conversations by topic by enabling a wiki page to be developed for every topic. Wikis differ from the social information spaces often described as groupware, computer-supported collaborative work systems or knowledge management systems in their lack of structure. There is no pre-defined structure to a wiki or the pages in a wiki (unless the wiki community decides there should be), and even if there is an initial structure to a wiki, that structure changes as the wiki community extends the wiki by adding and changing pages.

Common features of wikis

This section expands on our initial discussion to introduce the common features of wikis in more detail. These features are compared with the features of websites in Appendix A. Additional features available in some wikis are discussed in Chapter 7.

Wikis consist of pages accessible from a web browser

Wiki software creates pages and sites (collections of interlinked pages) that can be viewed in a web browser.

Like any other web resource, they include links to other pages, which can be both within and outside the wiki.

Pages can be edited with ease

The pages of a wiki are edited using a web browser on a computer connected to the Internet (or, in the case of wikis that reside in intranets, a corporate network). If any text needs to be marked as a link or displayed in a particular format, such as bold text or a heading, this can be done easily using either simple text formatting rules or a WYSIWYG editor. The text on the editing page shown in Figure 1.1b is formatted using the 'markup syntax' designed for the MediaWiki software. The user does not, however, need to know the markup language. They can simply select the text to be marked up and click on the formatting icon at the top of the edit window.

Links can be added with ease

The same mechanism for editing text is used to identify links, both internal and external to the wiki. A contributor simply includes the name of the link in the text as they are writing, and marks it up using the convention that is adopted by the wiki. These conventions provide simple ways to identify when a link is internal or external to the wiki. If the linked page is internal to the wiki but does not already exist, it is flagged for creation. Once the new text with the link is saved, clicking on the link allow the user to edit the newly created page. This process allows contributors to the wiki to create its structure, rather than having the structure imposed by another person.

Pages can be updated in real time

A change saved after editing a wiki page will be reflected in the published page. Most wikis display changes immediately, but some wikis will, if requested, hold changes pending authorisation.

Wikis are collectively edited

The original philosophy of wikis was that any person can edit any part of a wiki, by editing an existing page, or adding a new page. While restrictions can now be placed on editing in many wikis, the underlying concept that any page can be edited by many people means that the actual content of a wiki represents the collaborative work of a collection or community of authors rather than the work of one person. In pages authored by groups, individuals give up any rights to ownership of specific text in recognition of the collective work of the whole community of authors.

Wikis keep a history of changes

Almost all wikis keep track of changes. Older versions of a page can be viewed and even restored. In most wikis, the author of each version is recorded. Authors may be recorded by IP address, nickname, e-mail address or real name, depending on the wiki software and the registration rules and practices of the site. Figure 1.2 shows the revision history of the page displayed in Figure 1.1a.

Recent changes can be viewed

Many wikis contain a page or area in which the most recent changes to the wiki (i.e. to any page in the wiki) are displayed. This helps members of the wiki community to

Figure 1.2 Revision history for Wikipedia entry on wikis

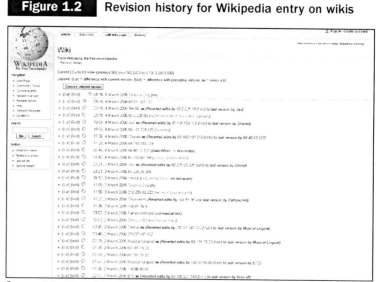

Source: *http://en.wikipedia.org/w/index.php?title=Wiki&action=history*

keep up to date with changes across the whole wiki and helps new members to get a feel for the issues that the wiki community is currently discussing.

Users can be alerted to change

Many wikis provide some sort of alerting mechanism that users can choose to use to notify them of changes. The two most common forms are integration with news aggregators, such as RSS and the provision of e-mail alerts or daily change summaries. News aggregators are used to alert a user to changes in a web page or site.[12]

Search and navigation

Most wikis provide some ability to search within the wiki. Navigation assistance is often provided in the text on the front page of the wiki or, in some cases, in a sidebar.

Simple permissions structure

Most wikis have a simple permissions structure based on permission to read what is in the wiki, to edit it, or to have the additional privileges of a wiki administrator. Some wikis enable these three levels to be applied to each page (and sometimes also collections of pages) as well as to the wiki as a whole. Differences in permission to read and contribute give rise to the distinction between public and private wikis. The additional privileges of wiki administrators include setting the permissions for reading and editing, and taking special editing actions, such as deleting or undeleting versions of pages.

Wiki philosophy

The features of wikis are derived from a set of principles established by Ward Cunningham, the inventor of the first wiki, the Portland Pattern Repository. Table 1.2 shows these principles as interpreted by Christian Wagner.[13]

While these principles underlie the technical design of wiki software, some social conventions have also guided the development of wikis. Critical to these is the notion of 'soft security'. The principles of soft security are summarised in the following terms at MeatballWiki:[14]

- *Assume good faith.* People are almost always trying to be helpful; so, we trust everyone, confident that occasional bad will be overwhelmed by the good.
- *Peer review.* Users, rather than software or [system administrators] moderate each other.
- *Forgive and forget.* Even well intentioned people make mistakes. They don't need to be permanent.

Table 1.2   Wiki design principles

Open	If a page is found to be incomplete or poorly organised, any reader can edit it as he/she sees fit.
Incremental	Pages can cite other pages, *including pages that have not been written yet.*
Organic	The structure and text content of the site is open to editing and evolution.
Mundane	A small number of (irregular) text conventions will provide access to the most useful (but limited) page markup.
Universal	The mechanisms of editing and organising are the same as those of writing so that any writer is automatically an editor and organiser.
Overt	The formatted (and printed) output will suggest the input required to reproduce it (e.g. location of the page).
Unified	Page names will be drawn from a flat space so that no additional context is required to interpret them.
Precise	Pages will be titled with sufficient precision to avoid most name clashes, typically by forming noun phrases.
Tolerant	Interpretable (even if undesirable) behaviour is preferred to error messages.
Observable	Activity within the site can be watched and reviewed by any other visitor to the site.
Convergent	Duplication can be discouraged or removed by finding and citing similar or related content.

Source: Wagner, C. (2004) 'Wiki: A technology for conversational knowledge management and group collaboration', *Communications of the Association for Information Systems* 13: 265–89. See: *http://cais.isworld.org/articles/ 13-19/default.asp?View=Journal&x=31&y=13* (accessed: 23 February 2006).

- *Limit damage.* When mistakes are made, minimise the damage.
- *Fair process.* The theory that being transparent and giving everyone a voice are essential management skills.

... Technology is only introduced to assist the people in their work. Because soft security relies entirely on social forces to maintain order, it remains not only adaptable to new threats, but tolerant in its responses. Conversely, encoded, programmatic ('hard') security is incapable of distinguishing attacks from mistakes, nor can it be argued with, nor can it be held accountable.

Soft security principles underlie the inclusion in wikis of an audit trail of changes, which enables peer review and the ability to reverse changes, which 'gives people the confidence to do anything knowing they cannot do permanent harm and that their mistakes can be forgotten'.[15]

Wikis are more than social software

There is more to wikis, then, than social software. Wikis may be viewed as technology, space, information and knowledge resources, philosophy, or even community. As a technology, wikis are software that permits many people to quickly and easily edit the same page using a web browser. (For the moment, authors access different copies of the page as they edit it, but wiki developers are aiming for simultaneous editing in the future.) Wiki pages are spaces that allow people to collaboratively share information and ideas, so wikis are also spaces for the social construction of knowledge. Because the contents of a wiki can be read by any authorised person – and, in many cases, by anyone using the World Wide Web – wikis are also information and knowledge resources. Wiki can also be considered to be a 'philosophy', in its ideal form, a view that the wisdom of many will always be superior to the thoughts of an individual, combined with a belief that systems should allow people to exchange their ideas quickly using simple technology. Furthermore, the word 'wiki' often conjures up something more than any of these points of view alone.[16] The collaborative nature of knowledge creation in a wiki is associated not just with creation of content but also with creation of community. The readers and contributors to a wiki are often considered a community[17] that defines and is defined by, the topics included in the wiki and the norms adopted for its use.

None of these points of view alone defines a wiki. While it is the software that distinguishes wikis from other types of collaboration space or information resource, a wiki needs content to exist, and the way in which content is developed draws on the philosophy of wikis (even if not in its pure form) and the notion of a group or community of authors. Figure 1.3 illustrates how wikis embody all of these points of view.

In this book, we are concerned not so much with wikis as social software or technology, but as 'social information spaces',[18] places where people can share ideas, knowledge and information simply and quickly regardless of their geographical location.

Figure 1.3   Wikis combine technology, space, information resource, philosophy and group or community

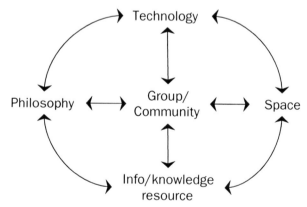

A *brief history of wikis*

The first wiki was the Portland Pattern Repository, developed by Ward Cunningham in 1995. The wiki was developed to support a relatively small community of software developers and others with an interest in 'extreme computing'. This wiki still exists today, in a much expanded form, as a resource for the wiki community as well as software developers with an interest in patterns, as the WikiWikiWeb.[19]

Given the success of the Portland Pattern Repository, wikis became popular among the software development and computing community, in particular. These wikis, although technically open to the public, tended to be developed and used by small communities. They became a virtual location for developing and expressing the community, as well as a resource for sharing ideas and information. The success of a wiki, it was found, was associated with the health of the community that it served. An inactive community meant a largely untended wiki with pages that remained incomplete or were out of date.

The desire to offer new features in wiki software led to the development of a number of different 'wiki engines', most of them open source[20] and available for free download. These early wiki engines, many of them still available today, required some technical knowledge to install, maintain and extend (even though they were still relatively simple by industry standards). Most of this software allowed rudimentary editing of web pages by contributors who were familiar with markup languages, but non-technical people did not find them particularly friendly. Thus, wikis tended to remain the domain of technical communities until the early twenty-first century.

MeatballWiki[21] was founded by Sunir Shah in 2000 to deal with issues associated with collaborative multimedia.

Ideas associated with developing and maintaining online communities were explored. Although MeatballWiki is not limited to wikis, the ideas developed there drew on contributors' experiences with wikis. This experience led to the creation of a number of pages about wikis and wiki technology, many of which are still maintained by the MeatballWiki community.

In the early 2000s, a number of other developments occurred. Jimmy Wales, the founder of Wikipedia and his colleague, Larry Sanger (now involved with the Digital Universe project),[22] after having experimented with Nupedia,[23] a web-based encyclopaedia, launched the Wikipedia project in January 2001. In December 2005, Wikipedia was reported to have more than 45,000 active contributors.[24] Wikis and the notion of communally developing websites, had been introduced to the general public, largely through news media articles about Wikipedia.

During the same period, a number of new wiki engines were launched and some of the older ones were given facelifts. Many of the new wiki engines were designed to be easy enough for people with limited technical skill to install. Some of these wiki engines simplified editing to the extent that contributors did not have to learn any markup language to add formatting or links to their text. The MediaWiki engine,[25] which underlies Wikipedia, was shown to have the ability to manage very large wikis. Consequently, it became popular with the developers of wikis for communities ranging from fan clubs to beer producers to golf players (see Chapter 2 for examples). As organisations' needs for software integration and security began to grow beyond what most open source packages could offer, so commercial software developed, notably Socialtext, then Confluence and, in 2005, JotSpot. Socialtext and JotSpot introduced the 'wiki appliance', a pre-configured server containing all the necessary software to run a wiki. It was now possible just to plug the server into your network and begin building wikis. Communities of software developers grew around many of these wiki engines, writing open source 'plug-ins' and 'extensions' to expand the functionality of the wikis and allow them to be integrated with other types of software, such as e-mail, blogs, calendars and project plans. More information about wiki software is provided in Chapter 7.

Another development was the growth in wiki hosting services. It is now possible to set up a wiki in a few minutes at a wiki farm or host site. Chapter 7 also provides more information about wiki hosting.

By the end of 2005, with a popular wiki capturing the public's imagination and the availability of a range of easy-to-use wiki engines, web appliances and wiki hosting, the conditions had been created for more widespread adoption of wikis. In August 2005, the information technology industry research company, the Gartner Group observed that wikis had passed the point at which expectations about their contributions was exaggerated and predicted that wikis and their use were two to five years away from reaching maturity.[26]

Wiki limitations, criticisms and controversies

The development of wikis has not been without controversy. Much of that controversy has surrounded the most public of wikis, Wikipedia, which has been criticised primarily for lack of authority and control over its entries.[27] Critics of Wikipedia point out that there is no guarantee that the people who edit a page are sufficiently expert in the topic or unbiased in their point of view to ensure that the content they add is accurate.[28] An alternative point of view holds that the ability of any reader to edit a page, and the sheer number of reader-contributors, provide an opportunity for many people to critically read, edit, extend and correct content.[29] Several authors have put Wikipedia to the test and discovered that it is more accurate than the critics expect. A blind comparison of entries in the electronic versions of Wikipedia and *Encyclopaedia Britannica*,[30] published by *Nature* in December 2005, found that there was little difference in the number of errors in science articles in the two encyclopaedias.[31] Several Wikipedia articles were, however, considered to be less well structured and less readable than the *Britannica* entries, perhaps a result of 'writing by committee'.

The ease with which other people can edit text has been described as '[the standard objection] ... if anybody can edit my text, then anybody can ruin my text'. The common fear of many newcomers to wikis is the fear that their work will be overwritten by someone else, or worse, be subject to spam or another form of vandalism. Enthusiastic contributors to wikis see the ability of others to change their text differently: they see it as an opportunity to add, to improve and to build knowledge. In some cases, users come to wikis with this attitude, in others they embrace this attitude to collaboration after some experience, but sometimes such an attitude needs to be built outside the wiki by developing trust and understanding in the process.

An interesting outcome of the collaborative writing process is that, regardless of the initial intentions behind establishment of a wiki, its content reflects the concerns of its users. 'Over time, the values, perspectives and opinions of its users can become embedded in a wiki'.[32] This gives each wiki a unique voice, which should be acknowledged by readers and contributors.

The temporal status of wikis can also be problematic. Unless the wiki community decides to lock the wiki, a wiki is always in a state of change. Entries in most wikis are 'works in progress' rather than final works.

Wikis can also appear to be chaotic environments. This is particularly true of some of the earlier wikis, although less so with most modern wikis that use contents lists, sidebars and other navigation tools to guide users. Nonetheless, because wiki structure is dynamically created as users create new pages, some management is needed to help users orient themselves (more about this in Chapter 8).

Wikis have been criticised for being ugly. Indeed, some members of the wiki community consider it important that content takes precedence over form and some early wikis in particular are undeniably ugly. Several writers have noted that non-technical wiki novices are put off by the appearance of some wikis. Recognising this, most modern wikis aim to achieve a balance between simplicity and attractiveness. Pages may display logos and use colours and formatting in ways which, while being simple to implement, are also attractive. Many wikis now allow global styles to be applied to 'lift' the look and feel of the wiki and its contents.

Finally, there is the thorny issue of intellectual property. The contributors to a wiki jointly own the content of the wiki. What are the implications for intellectual property rights when no single owner can be identified? Most public wikis deal with this problem by declaring the copyright to be owned by the collective and assigning rights to re-use material under a Creative Commons licence, which permits re-use under certain conditions.[33] But what happens if someone posts content that is already protected in a wiki? The hope is that this material will be deleted quickly by another user (and from the archive by the wiki administrator), but is this adequate protection, and in any case, who would be liable in the case of action being taken for breach of intellectual property? These issues are not easy to resolve and have not yet been addressed adequately. They are dealt with further in Chapter 8.

Wiki vocabulary

As you read about wikis you will come across some jargon developed by members of the early wiki community. Some of the more common terms are defined here.

- *Wiki.* (a) A collaboratively authored knowledge resource that is accessed and edited from a web browser using wiki software. When such a resource is available on the World Wide Web, it can be referred to as 'a collaboratively authored website' and 'an editable website'. (b) The software used to create a wiki site.

  In this book, when we use the word 'wiki', we will adopt the first of these definitions. When we are talking about the software used to create a wiki, we will describe it as 'wiki software' or a 'wiki engine'.

- *Front page.* The homepage of many wikis is called the 'front page'.

- *Public wikis.* Wikis that are open to members of the public to read and edit using a standard browser on the World Wide Web.

- *Private wikis* (also known as *gated wikis*). Wikis that are closed to members of the public. Private wikis may be developed by any group of individuals, across organisations, or within a single organisation. Membership is closed to all but registered members.

- *Wiki engine.* The software that produces the wiki and manages editing and other wiki functions.

- *Wiki farms.* The name given by the early wiki community to hosting services for wikis. Wikis can be set up either by running your own wiki software or by using the software and services provided across the Internet by wiki hosting services. Both the hosting service itself and the collection of wikis that run on the hosting service might be called a 'wiki farm'. An example is Wikia.[34]

- *Wiki gardening.* When wikis are open to editing by members of the public, they are also open to spam attacks and to the inclusion of malicious content. The process by which a wiki is regularly scanned for the spam, vandalism, or other changes that might merit a little cleaning up is known as 'wiki gardening'. In large wikis, such as Wikipedia, there might be teams of gardeners who monitor changes on several pages. In smaller wikis, this job might fall to the administrator of the wiki or the person who established a specific page. In most cases, wiki gardening requires a human being, although as wikis become more popular, automated facilities will assist this process.

- *Stub pages.* Blank pages or pages that contain only brief and preliminary information. Stub pages are used to provide structure to a wiki and to invite members of the public or wiki community to contribute information on topics that have not yet been developed.

- *Locked pages.* Pages that can only be edited by wiki administrators.

- *Frozen pages.* Pages whose content has been 'frozen' at a given date. Administrators can edit these pages, but changes are rarely made to the content once a page has been frozen.

- *CamelCase*. CamelCase is the practice of combining words by removing spaces and using a capital letter for the first letter of each word. CamelCase is a recognised naming convention in a number of fields.[35] It is used in many wiki engines to identify a wiki page. Combining words in CamelCase generates a link to an existing page of that name, or if no page exists, enables the user to create a page with that name. Not all wiki engines use CamelCase. MediaWiki, the software in which Wikipedia is created, prefers a different naming convention to identify links.

- *Wiki markup*. The system of symbols or annotations used in some wiki page editors to signify the formatting of certain text (e.g. headings or text to be shown in italics) and to identify links.

- *Sandbox*. A test area where users can practise editing the wiki.

Uses of wikis

If you think of a wiki as a space that can be quickly and easily edited by any (authorised) user, you can see that wikis lend themselves to many uses. In some ways, trying to explain the potential uses of wikis is a bit like trying to explain the potential uses of a large bundle of other types of software. Almost anything that can be written using a word processor can be written collaboratively in a wiki. And, as we will see in Chapter 7, wikis can also be used to collaborate in other formats, from whiteboards to spreadsheets.[36]

Our earlier discussion of how wikis differ from other types of social software points to some of the situations in which wikis can be used. They can be used in place of discussion forums, e-mail and blogs to permit collection of information and knowledge in a single place without the constraint of temporal order or the distraction of extraneous information. They are used in place of groupware, computer-supported collaborative work and knowledge management systems – when the knowledge to be shared and developed does not fit into the structures of these systems. They are used in place of static intranets to maintain documents, such as procedures manuals and technical documentation that can change quickly or benefit from being updated as new information comes to hand.

The public wikis that can be seen on the Internet represent only a fraction of the number of wikis that are in existence. Private wikis are popular in businesses and other organisations. They are used by groups of planners, researchers and colleagues working across organisations to plan meetings, develop information resources for their communities of practice, prepare conference programmes, write articles and prepare presentations, manage projects and, well, many other things besides. Members of the public do not see this part of the wiki universe, which usually resides on secure sites away from the possibility of spam or vandalism, and is maintained by small or relatively small communities of people who trust each other to follow principles similar to Meatball's soft security principles as they jointly complete their wiki-supported projects.

Indeed, wikis can be used by any group of people with the need or desire to collaborate or to 'socially construct' knowledge. Wikis can be used to prepare 'published' works, such as an Internet encyclopaedia or a rough draft of a document that will be published elsewhere (for example, this book). A wiki can be developed to gather and disseminate information for an indefinite period of time, or it can be put in place quickly to address an ad hoc problem (for example, Wagner describes a scenario in which a group of troubleshooters based in different locations needs to diagnose and resolve a series of manufacturing failures[37]). It has even been suggested that wikis can be used as a tool for continuous learning and increased autonomy among members of the intelligence community.[38]

We end this introductory chapter with some examples of uses to which wikis have been put. Chapters 2, 4, 5 and 6 provide more detail and more examples.

Reference works

The popularity of Wikipedia underlines how successful wikis can be for the development of reference works that draw on the collective knowledge of a group (large or small) of contributors. Wikis have also been developed as smaller reference works in specific subject areas; in addition, the reference format is being used in private wikis that act as staff manuals and other information of the kind that might be found on an organisation's intranet.

Websites for communities of practice, hobbyists and other interest groups

Public wikis are frequently used to jointly author websites for communities of practice, hobbyists and other interest groups. The communities that read and contribute to these wikis range in size from small groups of friends and colleagues who are well known to one another, to larger groups who form a community as they come to know each other online. There are many small community wikis covering quite specific topics, such as specific sports, books, religions and philosophies; these wikis form the long tail of the wiki universe. The larger community wikis can be rather like vibrant public open spaces to visit; a good example is the *Star Trek* fan site, Memory Alpha,[39] reviewed in Chapter 2.

Technical documentation and standards

Wikis are being used to draft technical documentation and standards, particularly where members of a standards development team are based in different geographical locations. They are also being used to prepare system documentation. An excellent example of public system documentation is that of Mozilla, the provider of the Firefox web browser, where members of the public contribute to Mozilla product documentation.[40] Some companies use wikis to develop documentation for their internal information systems, where users contribute documentation and correct existing material as they learn to use the systems.

Directories and lists

Another common use of wikis is shared creation of directories and lists. The most widely cited of these are the directories and lists of wikis and wiki software reviewed in Chapter 3, but wikis are also used by students and researchers to create annotated bibliographies, and within organisations to develop lists, such as staff lists, lists of job vacancies and suggestions.

Resource sharing

Some wikis extend their directories and lists into catalogues that enable sharing of resources. PlanetMath,[41] reviewed in

Chapter 2, includes mathematical expositions. Several US state and local government entities have combined with Harvard and MIT to develop the Government Open Code Collaborative (GOCC)[42] to share, at no cost, computer code developed by the entities.

News reports

As we will see in Chapter 2, wikis can be used to create news reports that draw on many points of view. They can be used to develop public news reports or reports of events that take place in schools and other organisations.

Conferences and events

Some groups use wikis to plan conferences or meetings and to build on ideas or contacts that were initially developed at conferences or meetings. An example of this use is the Blogwalk Wiki,[43] a wiki that was used during 2005 to share information about Blogwalk meetings throughout the world. Features include information about participants, including photographs in some cases, and participants' own responses to invitations to attend. Suter et al.[44] describe the 'San Diego Experiment' in which a number of types of software were used to augment participants' experience and social exchange at a conference. The audience was able to use a wiki to comment on a presentation, during the presentation. Boyd[45] describes a similar use throughout a workshop attended by 30 people. He notes that the participants quickly learnt to use wikis to capture 'their own streams of consciousness or the comments of others'.

Collaboration on projects and in committees

A common organisational use of wikis is project support. While wikis cannot (at least for the moment) replace project management systems, they are often used to support the sharing of ideas, resources, plans and schedules. Documents can be jointly produced within the wiki or made available as attachments to the wiki. Angeles describes how wikis have been used for documentation by Lucent Technologies, including preparation of meeting notes, product specification gathering notes, product requirements documents, project deliverables, content audits, technical documentation and style guides.[46] Wikis can be used by teams of students as well as business and research teams.

Wikis are used by committees to develop agendas (every member of the committee may be able to add an item to an agenda), to exchange ideas and comment on issues without the need to meet, and for general coordination of the Committee. The 2004 web pages of the California Interagency Watershed Mapping Committee wiki give an indication of the scope that a Committee wiki might cover.[47]

Surveys

Wikis can be combined with other tools to gather detailed comments and opinions for surveys. The ACM (an international professional body for computing professionals) used a wiki to select 20 out-of-print books from a list of 403 nominations, to be digitised and made available to an audience that would not otherwise have access to them. A wiki page was established for each nominated book and members used the pages to write vignettes about the book and its influence. They were then asked to vote for books to be digitised, drawing on comments made by all members in the wiki.

Other shared authoring projects

All of the uses that have been described so far involve shared authoring. Some other shared authoring projects include projects in which students or closed communities of colleagues have developed encyclopaedia entries to be posted, once complete, in Wikipedia; the joint authoring of public statements for publication on the Web or in newspapers; and the joint authoring of letters to politicians. Chapter 6 provides examples of several uses of wikis in creative writing courses. Lawrence Lessig, the author of *Code and Other Laws of Cyberspace* asked the public to contribute to the second edition of his book using a wiki.[48] He has now created the Anti-Lessig Reader with the aim 'to build a collection of content that criticises my work'.[49]

Website development

Wiki software also provides a quick and simple way to publish to the Web. An example of a wiki-generated website is the site developed by the Bach-Academie of Montreal to publicise a series of concerts. The musicians themselves added details to the wiki, which was then published on the Web.[50]

Personal wikis

The simple editing and web publication capabilities of wikis have led some individuals to use wiki software to develop their own websites, or in private mode, as notepads or drafting spaces that they can access at any time from any

Internet-connected computer at any location. The term 'personal wiki', however, is really an oxymoron. While wiki software can be used to create personal websites and personal pages, anything created in this way is not a wiki because it cannot be edited by anyone other than its creator.

Notes

1. Many thanks to Guy Fraser, Stefano Renzi, Marco Marlia and Maria Luisa Nigrelli for their critical reading and positive contributions to this chapter.

2. Suter, V., Alexander, B. and Kaplan, P. (2005) 'The future of FTF'. *EDUCAUSE Review* 40(1); available at: *http:// www.educause.edu/apps/er/erm05/erm0514.asp?bhcp=0511* (accessed: 3 January 2006) – suggest that the term 'social software' has been used in three different ways: 'tool (for augmenting human social and collaborative abilities) ... medium (for facilitation social connection and information interchange ... and ecology (for enabling a system of people, practices, values and technologies in a particular local environment'. While subtly different, these three uses all acknowledge that social software enables certain forms of human social behaviour. Our definition tries to capture this commonality. An excellent history of social software has been written by Christopher Allen: Allen C. (2004) 'Tracing the evolution of social software', *Life with Alacrity*; available at: *http://www.lifewithalacrity.com/2004/10/tracing_the_evo.html* (accessed: 25 January 2006).

3. Shirky, C. (2003) 'Social software and the politics of groups', *Clay Shirky's Writings about the Internet*; available at: *http://www.shirky.com/writings/group_politics.html* (accessed: 28 February 2006). Shirky discusses the strengths and weaknesses of this definition and expands on the notion in Shirky, C. (2003) 'A group is its own worst enemy', *Clay Shirky's Writings about the Internet*; available at: *http://www.shirky.com/writings/group_enemy.html* (accessed: 28 February 2006).

4. Hammond, T., Hannay, T., Lund, B. and Scott, J. (2005) 'Social bookmarking tools (I): A general review', *D-Lib Magazine* 11(4); available at: *http://www.dlib.org/dlib/april05/hammond/04hammond.html* (accessed: 23 January 2006; Millen, D., Feiberg, J. and Kerr, B. (2005) 'Social bookmarking in the enterprise', *ACM Queue* 3(9): 28–35; available from: *http://acmqueue.com/modules.php?name=Content&pa=showpage&pid=344* (accessed: 3 January 2006).

5. Boyd, S. (2004) 'Wicked (good) wikis', *Darwin*; available at: *http://www.darwinmag.com/read/020104/boyd.html* (accessed: 6 September 2005).

6. Frequently cited examples are the shared photograph site, flickr (*http://www.flickr.com*) and the social bookmarking site, delicious (*http://del.icio.us*).

7. Delio, M. (2005) 'Enterprise collaboration with blogs and wikis', *Infoworld*; available at: *http://www.infoworld.com/article/05/03/25/13FEblogwiki_1.html* (accessed: 11 February 2005).

8. In this book, we follow the convention of using lower case when we referring to wikis in general. We reserve uppercase for the names of specific wikis. The first wiki, the Portland Pattern Repository, now known as *WikiWikiWeb* (*http://c2.com/cgi/wiki*), is sometimes also called *Wiki*.

9. Eco, U. (2006) 'Come copiare da Internet', *L'espresso*; available at: *http://www.espressonline.it/eol/free/jsp/detail.jsp?m1s=o&m2s=null&idCategory=4789&idContent=1252511* (accessed: 19 January 2006).

10. What You See is What You Get.

11. For an overview of how wikis got their name, see the Wikipedia definition at: *http://en.wikipedia.org/wiki/Wiki*.

12. For more information, see Bricklin, D. S. (2006) 'What is RSS?'; available at: *http://whatis.techtarget.com/definition/0,289893,sid289899_gci1088619,1088600.html* (accessed: 13 January 2006).

13. Wagner, C. (2004) 'Wiki: A technology for conversational knowledge management and group collaboration', *Communications of the Association for Information Systems* 13: 265–89; available at: *http://cais.isworld.org/articles/*

13–19/default.asp?View=Journal&x=31&y=13 (accessed: 23 February 2006).

14. Meatball (2006) 'Soft Security'; available at: *http://usemod.com/ cgi-bin/mb.pl?SoftSecurity* (page dated 15 January 2006; accessed: 1 March 2006).

15. Ibid.

16. MeatballWiki has a fascinating discussion of what 'wiki' actually means, setting the various definitions and uses of the word 'wiki' in the context of the growth of wikis. This is not a site for wiki novices, but once you have a bit of experience, you might enjoy: Meatball, 'WhatIsaWiki'; available at: *http://www.usemod.com/cgi-bin/mb.pl?WhatIsaWiki* (page dated 20:30, 29 January 2006; accessed: 2 February 2006).

17. Wellman, B. (2005) 'Community: From neighborhood to network', *Communications of the ACM* 48(10): 53–5.

18. Fisher, D. (2003) 'Studying social information spaces', in C. Lueg and D. Fisher (eds) *From Usenet to CoWebs*. London: Springer-Verlag; pp. 3–19.

19. See: *www.c2.com/cgi/wiki*.

20. Open source software is software whose source code (the program) is open to all, without the need to pay a fee.

21. See: *http://www.usemod.com/cgi-bin/mb.pl?MeatballWiki*.

22. See: *http://www.digitaluniverse.net*.

23. See the Wikipedia definition of Nupedia at: *http://en.wikipedia.org/wiki/Nupedia* (page dated 03:11, 4 March 2006; accessed: 5 March 2006).

24. Terdiman, D. (2005) 'Wikipedia alternative aims to be 'PBS of the web', *CNET News.com*; available at: *http://news.com.com/Wikipedia+alternative+aims+to+be+PBS+of+the+Web/2100-1038_3-5999200.html* (accessed: 10 January 2006).

25. See: *http://www.mediawiki.org/*.

26. Fenn, J. and Linden, A. (2005) *Gartner's Hype Cycle Special Report for 2005*. Stamford, CT: Gartner Group.

27. Wikipedia even devotes an entry to responding to criticisms: Wikipedia, 'Wikipedia: Replies to Common Objections': *http://en.wikipedia.org/wiki/Wikipedia:Replies_to_common_objections* (page dated 13:40, 12 January 2006; accessed: 13 January 2006).

28. Holders of this point of view include Robert McHenry, a former editor in chief of *Encyclopaedia Britannica*: McHenry, R. (2004) 'The Faith-Based Encyclopedia'; available at: *http://www.techcentralstation.com/111504A.html* (accessed: 13 January 2006).

29. A scholarly analysis of why this might be so can be found in Ciffolilli, A. (2003) 'Phantom authority, self-selective recruitment and retention of members in virtual communities: The case of Wikipedia', *First Monday* 8(12); available at: *http://firstmonday.org/issues/issue8_12/ciffolilli* (accessed: 13 January 2006).

30. See: *http://www.britannica.com*.

31. Giles, J. (2005) 'Internet encyclopaedias go head to head', *Nature* 438: 900–1; available at: *http://www.nature.com/nature/journal/v438/n7070/pdf/438900a.pdf*. The comparison methodology and results table are available online at: *www.nature.com/news/2005/051212/multimedia/438900a_m1.html* (accessed: 13 January 2006).

32. EDUCAUSE Learning Initiative (2005) 'Seven things you should know about wikis'; available at: *http://www.educause.edu/ir/library/pdf/ELI7004.pdf* (accessed: 3 January 2006).

33. See: *http://creativecommons.org*.

34. See: *http://www.wikia.com*.

35. See the Wikipedia definition of CamelCase at: *http://en.wikipedia.org/wiki/CamelCase* (page dated 02:37, 19 January 2006; accessed: 19 January 2006).

36. At the time of writing, Dan Bricklin, the inventor of the first PC spreadsheet was about to launch a wiki spreadsheet: Terdiman, D. (2006) 'Software pioneer Bricklin tackles wikis', *CNET News.com*, 17 February; available at: *http://news.com.com/Software+pioneer+Bricklin+tackles+wikis/2100-1032_3-6040867.html* (accessed: 17 February 2006).

37. Wagner, op. cit.

38. Andrus, D. C. (2005) 'The wiki and the blog: toward a complex adaptive intelligence community'; available at: *http://papers.ssrn.com/sol3/papers.cfm?abstract_id=755904* (accessed: 28 February 2006).

39. See: *http://memory-alpha.org.*
40. See: *http://kb.mozillazine.org.*
41. See: *http://planetmath.org.*
42. See: *http://www.gocc.gov.*
43. See: *http://blogwalk.interdependent.biz/wikka.php?wakka=HomePage.*
44. Suter et al. (2005) op cit.
45. Boyd, S. (2004b) op cit.
46. Angeles, M. (2004) 'Using a wiki for documentation and collaborative authoring'; available at: *http://www.llrx.com/features/librarywikis.htm* (accessed: 6 September 2005).
47. See: *http://cain.nbii.org/calwater/wiki* (accessed: 20 January 2006).
48. Lessig, L. (2005) 'Codebook'; available at: *http://codebook.jot.com* (accessed: 27 February 2006).
49. Lessig, L. (2006) 'Anti-Lessig Reader'; available at: *http://wiki.lessig.org/index.php/Anti-Lessig_Reader* (page dated 18:04, 11 February 2006; accessed: 27 February 2006).
50. See: *http://www.bach-academie-de-montreal.com/.*

Wikis as information sources
Jane Klobas

Wikis can act as information sources in public, educational and business situations. This chapter concentrates on wikis as public information sources, that is, wikis that are publicly available on the World Wide Web.

Like other Web resources, wikis can be useful sources of information. And, like other Web resources, they can also misinform, mislead, infuriate and even offend their readers. This chapter looks at the advantages and problems of wikis as sources of information. It contains advice about evaluating web resources in general, and wikis in particular. It also includes examples of wikis as information resources. The examples do not include websites that are built using wiki engines but are closed for editing. Instead, we look at wikis themselves, sites that are built and maintained through collaborative authoring where authors use their web browsers to edit content.

Advantages and problems of wikis as information sources

Accuracy, reach and depth are three potential qualities of jointly authored resources. When 'many eyeballs' read and review the same material, they are able to identify and correct more errors than a single author.[1] Together, a group of authors knows more than a single author; a collaboratively developed resource can, therefore, cover more topics or more aspects of a topic than a resource developed by one person working alone. When members of a collaborating team share different areas of expertise, the team can also deal with a range of topics or aspects of a topic in more depth than a single author.

Wikis also have the advantage that they can be developed quickly. Any Internet-connected computer anywhere in the world can be used to contribute at any time to a public wiki. Breaking news stories and sites that provide information for disaster response can be updated as soon as information comes to hand, making wikis a potentially excellent resource for up-to-the-minute information.

The ability to track revisions over time has an advantage that is unique to wikis. It is possible to track the development of a news story or of an idea or topic by tracking through the revisions.

There are, however, threats to the ability of wikis to live up to their potential. Accuracy, reach and depth can only be achieved when the authors have expertise in the topics about which they are writing, and the goodwill to contribute in the spirit of the wiki community to which they are contributing. Currency relies on ongoing contributions, even after an immediate crisis or story has broken. Good administration is needed to identify when a topic is closed and to date stamp and lock a page for historical purposes.

The changing nature of wiki pages can be frustrating when they are used as information sources. Because search engines do not work on live web pages but on indexes that periodically scan the web, the terms contained in the index do not always match the words that appear on the current version of a web page. Wikis tend to change more often than other web pages, so the effect of indexing delays can be more pronounced.

A combination of technical and management issues can threaten the ability of wikis to be effective sources of information. Most wiki engines allow restriction of editing rights to registered users, but many wikis are, either for technical reasons or because of decisions made by the wiki's administrators, open for public editing. However, the same mechanism that leaves a wiki open to any member of the public to edit without registration enables automated addition by web bots[2] of spam or other undesirable content. When editing is open and specific action is not taken to prevent malicious attacks, the informational content of a wiki can be replaced by irrelevant content. Some wikis get around this problem by using editors who regularly review and, where necessary, correct each page. Increasingly, however, wikis require contributors to register before making a contribution. Some wiki purists see required registration as an attack on the open philosophy of wikis. The risk, when using wikis maintained by communities that hold this point of view, is that a page of irrelevant text may have replaced a page that a user is seeking. Fortunately, the feature to track revisions provided by most wikis also allows a user to track back to the page with the sought information and even to restore it.

But, then, the ability to restore an earlier version of a page brings its own problems. The larger and more open the community that contributes to a wiki, the more likely that the wiki will fall prone to 'edit wars' (also known as 'revert wars'). Edit wars occur when two or more contributors with different points of view – about content, or about style or expression – dispute which version of a page should be the 'definitive' version. At its extreme, an edit war can see each contributor reverting a page to the version that they wrote, one after the other, until another person, such as an editor or higher level wiki administrator steps in.

Not all wikis are designed with navigation in mind, and finding information within a wiki often relies on the quality of the wiki's search engine and the navigation tools that have been added manually by its authors. The most common navigation tool is a contents list on the front page or at the top of an individual page. Contents lists are notably absent from older wikis in particular. (The front page of the first wiki, WikiWikiWeb, for example, provides guidance for new users, but instructs users to use the FindPage facility – a somewhat unsophisticated search engine on a separate page – or browse by category to find information on a specific topic.)[3] Navigation of wikis without contents lists requires some patience and persistence, or experience with the site.

A lesser problem, but one that can affect users' perceptions of a wiki as an authoritative information resource, is visual appeal. Not all wiki engines encourage attention to the visual appeal of the pages that are produced, so wikis of different kinds and wikis on different subjects created using the same wiki engine tend to look much the same. This is particularly true of the open source wiki engines which are frequently used to develop public wikis.

Evaluating wikis as sources of information

The advantages and problems of wikis as information sources suggest a number of criteria for evaluation. In addition, we need to evaluate wikis as we would any other Web-based information resource. In her book, *Weblogs and Libraries*, Anne Clyde provided a comprehensive set of criteria for evaluating blogs, including general criteria for evaluating Web-based information resources.[4] These criteria form the basis of the discussion included in this chapter. Appendix B contains a list of evaluation questions based on Anne Clyde's list and this discussion.

Criteria for assessing information content

Wikis should first be evaluated along the primary dimensions for evaluation of any source of information. The most important of these are summarised here.

- *Purpose.* It is useful to know why a wiki was developed and who the intended users or readers are. Some wikis are designed as resources for the public while others are designed for experts in a specific field. The more closely aligned the purpose of a wiki is to the needs of the information seeker, the more likely the information provided will meet those needs.

- *Scope and coverage.* In addition to purpose, information about the scope and coverage of a wiki can help determine the likelihood that the wiki will meet a user's information needs. Relevant issues might include the geographic coverage, any limitations by time and the inclusion or exclusion of certain types of content. Coverage also includes the depth with which issues are covered: does the wiki aim to provide summaries and overviews or in-depth analyses? Links and references to additional resources can add to the coverage of a wiki.

- *Authority.* Authority of a wiki, as with any information source, is a critical dimension for evaluation. There may be different layers of authority, including the authority of the authors of the wiki, but extending also to the authority of the organisation, individual or group that established the wiki and the structure that is used to manage and maintain it. Authority can also be enhanced by systems of editorial or peer review. Some guidance to authority might be provided through inclusion of the wiki in a directory or reference work that selects resources on the basis of their quality. Most wiki engines include features that assist with evaluation of the authority of a wiki. These include the ability to track changes, to attribute changes to a specific person and even to require authors and editors to register with their real names or e-mail addresses.

- *Accuracy*. Another critical evaluative dimension is accuracy. While accuracy may be verified by comparing the content of a wiki with content available in other sources, this is not always practical. Look for independent articles and research that examine accuracy. Examine the wiki for the point of view that it expounds and any potential bias. Does the wiki refer to sources where relevant? Within the wiki, some indication of accuracy might be found in the quality of the writing and in the presence or absence of spelling and grammatical errors.

- *Currency*. An information source also needs to be up to date. This requires attention to both the textual information and photographic and other graphical content. Information about the date of the latest update helps to evaluate currency. Because wikis can change several times in a single day, information about the time of the latest update, as well as the date, is provided on many wikis.

Criteria for assessing features of online resources

Each generic form of information resource (e.g. book, journal, audio tape or website) has a set of criteria specific to that type of resource. The criteria listed here are those for evaluation of online resources in general, including websites, blogs and wikis. The commentary adapts these criteria specifically for wikis.

- *Format.* The format of an online resource includes the way it is presented to the user, most notably the organisation of each page and the structure of the resource as a whole. The format of a wiki should be compatible with the purpose of the wiki, its intended audience and the content that it covers. Thus, a wiki that is intended to be an encyclopaedia written for members of the public should be laid out and structured in such a way that it is easy for readers to find entries on topics and to follow links to related entries.

- *Appearance.* Users of online resources are influenced by their appearance. Appearance includes layout issues, such as fonts, colours and amount and location of white space, contents lists, search facilities and links. Appearance can give a first impression of authority, accuracy and suitability for a specific audience. For example, an apparently chaotic layout may indicate that a wiki has been developed for a specific community and is not particularly appropriate for general readers.

- *Navigation.* The ability to navigate within an online resource is critical to the ability to find information in the resource. Navigation aids can include contents lists, regularly updated site maps, classification schemes with links that allow users to browse for information in a network or hierarchy of relationships, and search engines.

- *Links.* The quality of links is important in an online resource. They should be accurate, relevant and up to date. Each link should consist of, or be accompanied by, an informative description of where the link leads. A convention for distinguishing links to content within a wiki from content in external sites can help readers make decisions about which links to follow.

- *User needs.* In addition to general issues about purpose, scope and coverage, specific user needs may also need to be addressed in an online resource. These include suitable language or languages and accessibility to people with problems with vision and sound. In some cases, access to certain content within a wiki may be limited to registered users; will this limit the wiki's usefulness for your purposes?

- *Technical aspects.* A wiki should work well in all browsers likely to be used by members of its audience. As with any online resource, it should load quickly onto the browser, across all types of connection that members of the audience are likely to be using, and be available at all times of the day, seven days a week. Additional technical issues that directly affect the user's experience include the length of each page and the ability to print the page in a suitable format.

Criteria specific to evaluation of wikis

This section considers some specific issues associated with evaluation of wikis. These need to be considered along with the generic criteria for evaluation of information sources and online information sources.

- *Reliability.* Reliability is an issue of particular importance for evaluation of wikis. The frequency with which a wiki changes should be appropriate to its purpose, scope and audience; for example, a wiki news service needs to be updated as events on which it is reporting change, while some encyclopaedia entries may remain unchanged for some time after the entry has become stable. Changes may be minor (for example, correction of typographical errors) or may affect the informational content of the wiki. Changes to content should improve the content. Edit wars, spam and vandalism, however, threaten this principle, so evaluation of a wiki may need to include evaluation of editorial policies for resolution of disputes about content, and should include examination of technical and managerial strategies for dealing with spam and vandalism.

■ *Features.* Finally, it is useful to consider how well a specific wiki has implemented the features available in wiki software. For example, are mechanisms for annotating changes to content (e.g. as minor changes) implemented and used, does the wiki enable discussion of the content of each page on a separate page rather than on the page itself, and does it include a mechanism for setting up an RSS or Atom feed that will alert users to changes in content?

Some examples of wikis

Wikis are particularly well suited to production of works that involve information gathered from several sources and information that is updated over time. The examples included in this section all have these characteristics. They are examined under the headings: reference works; directories, indexes and lists; wikis for disaster response; wikis in news reporting; community and interest group wikis; wikis about wikis; and information technology wikis. This list warrants a disclaimer: some of the examples cited here may have changed or even been withdrawn by the time you read this text. Chapter 3 provides some guidance for finding wikis if you are looking for additional examples.

Reference works

The 'collective intelligence' capabilities of wikis make them ideal for the development of reference works. Wiki-based reference works do not have a date of completion (after which the information within them becomes dated); instead, they are continually under development.

The most well-known wiki reference works are managed under the auspices of the Wikimedia Foundation, a non-profit foundation 'dedicated to encouraging the growth, development and distribution of free, multilingual content and to providing the full content of these wiki-based projects to the public free of charge'.[5] The Foundation has a small board of trustees chaired by Jimmy Wales, the founder of Wikipedia and the Wikimedia Foundation. Reference works in the Wikimedia stable in January 2006 were: Wikipedia, an encyclopaedia; Wiktionary, a multilingual dictionary and thesaurus; Wikiquote,[6] a dictionary of quotations; and Wikispecies,[7] a species directory. This section contains brief reviews of Wikipedia and Wiktionary, as well as references to alternatives and some other popular wiki reference applications.

Wikipedia

http://www.wikipedia.org

Wikipedia is an encyclopaedia available on the World Wide Web.[8] Contributions are open to any Web user[9] and the content may be used freely, provided the copyright holder is acknowledged appropriately and the content is retained under the GNU Free Documentation License.[10] By 1 January 2006, there were more than 210 different language editions of Wikipedia, although some, such as Cheyenne, had only a handful of entries.[11] The largest edition was the English language edition with more than 900,000 entries.[12] Coverage varies, according to the interest of contributors, but there appears to be wider and more up-to-date coverage of topics in Wikipedia than in other encyclopaedia.[13] The introduction to the entry on wikis appears in Figure 1.1b.

Wiktionary

http://en.wiktionary.org

While Wikipedia is an encyclopaedia, with detailed entries that often consider the history and development of a topic, Wiktionary provides simple definitions and basic etymology. On 13 January 2006, the entry for wiki in Wiktionary said, simply, 'Any website based on any kind of Wiki software which enables users to *quickly* add to, edit and delete from the site's content' while the Wikipedia entry on wikis contained more than 2,500 words defining wikis, describing how they work and detailing their history. In January 2006, Wiktionary had entries in 45 languages. There were more than 110,000 entries in English.

Wikinfo (Internet-Encyclopedia)

http://www.internet-encyclopedia.org

Wikinfo, a 'multilingual open content encyclopaedia' was launched in July 2003 by Fred Bauder, as a 'fork' of Wikipedia. There were more than 34,000 pages in January

2006. Many of the articles are drawn from articles in Wikipedia, but Wikinfo has a different editorial policy so the articles do differ. Unlike Wikipedia, which adopts a 'neutral point of view',[14] the main article on each subject in Wikinfo adopts a 'sympathetic point of view'.[15] Alternative points of view can be added, usually as articles linked to the main article. Some topics do not appear in Wikinfo, for example, there are no entries for current and recent US presidents, although there is an article about the role of 'president' and entries for Theodore Roosevelt and Charles de Gaulle. There are relatively few contributors to Wikinfo, and all must register.

Digital Universe

http://www.digitaluniverse.net

The Digital Universe was launched early in 2006 with the vision to provide 'an online knowledge repository and community of knowledge-building collaborators, held in the public trust' by offering 'the tools and the interactivity to encourage an active lifelong learning process' and organising information and offering 'knowledge tools to empower an informed citizenry'.[16] The Digital Universe is structured and managed differently from Wikipedia. Initial plans are that each major subject area is accessed via a portal developed under the guidance of a 'steward'. The portal will provide access to resources contributed by experts and peer-reviewed as well as resources contributed by members of the public. The goal is to make Digital Universe more than an encyclopaedia, but a multimedia resource that might include video, news reports and public domain books, supported by discussion and chat.[17] Digital Universe has been launched with high ideals and great ambition. It will take some time before we will know if its vision will be achieved.

Wikitravel

http://wikitravel.org

Wikitravel is a relatively new wiki. It aims to develop a world travel guide through the contributions of travellers. In January 2006, there were more than 10,000 entries in several languages.

The Open Guide to London

http://london.openguides.org

The Open Guide to London is the biggest of several city guides developed as part of the Open Guides Project.[18] In many ways, it is a typical city guide. It contains lists and reviews of places to sleep, eat and drink (indeed, beer is a speciality of this guide, which began as the *grubstreet* guide to London pubs).[19] It has information on tube stations, bus routes, supermarkets, meeting venues and other facilities. What sets this (and the other wiki Open Guides) apart from other guides is that each page includes a postal code and spatial grid coordinates that allow users to explore a location, e.g. to locate pubs near tube stations or hotels near meeting venues. The Open Guide to London is well organised and mostly up to date, and the pub reviews in particular are written in a frank and friendly style. Pages vary, but the structure is similar. Expect information and comment similar to the short entry shown in Figure 2.1.

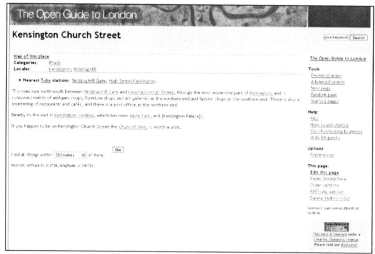

Figure 2.1 The Open Guide to London: Kensington Church Street entry

Source: *http://london.openguides.org/index.cgi?Kensington_Church_Street*

Directories, indexes, lists and digital libraries

Annotated bibliographies, lists of readings and references and a range of specialist directories and indexes are also available in wiki format. Resources are directly available from some of these sites, making them digital libraries. Many of these sites are provided as part of the larger website or wiki of a community or group, but they are worth noting separately because of their value as information sources. On the down side, these tools can be difficult to find because few of them are searchable independently of the larger wiki within which they sit.

New Zealand Open Source Society Case Studies

http://nzoss.org.nz/wiki/CaseStudies

The New Zealand Open Source Society maintains a suite of wikis suitable for people new to open source software as well as experts. Among the wikis is an annotated list of the case studies of business and educational organisations that are using open source software. Like any open wiki, readers and users can add to this list.

The Choral Public Domain Library

http://www.cpdl.org/wiki

This wiki is both a directory to and a library of sheet music freely available on the Web. More than 7,500 scores were available, some in multiple editions, in January 2006.[20]

Wikisource

http://wikisource.org

See below.

Wikibooks

http://www.wikibooks.org

The Wikimedia Foundation is also developing digital libraries. Wikisource, described as 'The Free Library'[21] is a collection of previously published material. The available texts include works of fiction and poetry that are no longer covered by copyright, religious texts, ancient and classical works, speeches, election data from several countries and national anthems. Wikibooks is a project for collaborative writing of textbooks and other works of non-fiction. The contents are made available under the GNU Free Documentation License.[22] Specific information about the educational potential of Wikibooks is given Chapter 6.

Wikis for disaster response

Unlike printed reference works, wiki reference tools can be developed very quickly. The tools can be developed by individuals and groups working almost simultaneously in different locations. These characteristics of wikis are particularly valuable in constructing resources in response to disasters, such as hurricanes, floods and war.

Radio Reference Hurricane Rita Wiki

http://www.radioreference.com/wiki/index.php/Hurricane_Rita

Hurricane Rita was one of the most intense hurricanes ever recorded. It hit the Gulf of Mexico in late September 2005. Attempts to respond to the effects of the hurricane demonstrated how difficult it is to maintain communications during and in the days following, a natural disaster, even in developed countries. Radio Reference 'is the world's largest radio communications reference website'.[23] The site includes a large wiki where subscribers maintain lists of radio frequencies, monitoring information and information about software. The Radio Reference community developed the Hurricane Rita wiki on 22 September 2005 to record and share information about the radio frequencies in use as the hurricane hit the USA. An extract from the wiki appears in Figure 2.2.

Wikis in news reporting

Wikis are being used to report and update breaking news. Because many people can contribute to a wiki news report, information from people who experience an event in different locations and those who see it from different points of view can be gathered quickly in a single article. The

Figure 2.2   Radio frequencies for Hurricane Rita
(RadioReference.com)

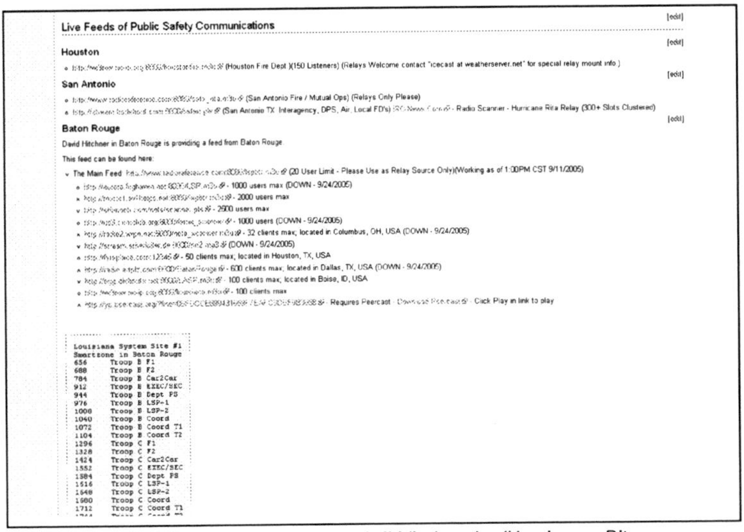

Source: *http://www.radioreference.com/wiki/index.php/Hurricane_Rita*

development of a story over time can be followed by tracking the revisions to the web page.

Wikinews

http://www.wikinews.org

This is the largest wiki news service and another project under the banner of the Wikimedia Foundation. Contributors are 'citizen journalists',[24] members of the public who may provide eyewitness accounts or draw (with acknowledgment) on other news sources. All content is made available 'for free distribution and use' under a Creative Commons licence.

Figure 2.3 shows a screen from the Wikinews report of the London bomb attacks on 7 July 2005. The attacks were first reported in a few lines just after the first explosion was heard at 08:49. In the 12 hours after the attacks, the report was updated or edited 543 times. If you track the changes in news content,[25] a picture emerges of how information about

Figure 2.3   Wikinews: 'Coordinated terrorist attack hits London'

Source: *http://en.wikinews.org/w/index.php?title=Coordinated_terrorist_attack_hits_London*

a disaster changes quickly as initial confusion gives way to increasing clarity.

Wikis about wikis

Until recently, wikis were the domain of enthusiasts. These wikis contain technical information about how to build wikis, discussions about wiki technology and applications and directories and finding tools for wikis. Some also contain advice about how to develop the communities that maintain wikis and how to manage tricky issues, such as permissions and security.

WikiWikiWeb

http://www.c2.com/cgi/wiki

As we mentioned in Chapter 1, the first wiki, the Portland Pattern Repository, is known as WikiWikiWeb. The focus of the wiki is people, projects and patterns in software development. The nature of wikis themselves falls within this scope and the WikiWikiWeb contains much useful information about wikis. It takes some time to get used to navigating this wiki, but help for newcomers is available on the Starting Points page.[26] There is a link to a search page at the bottom of each wiki page.

MeatballWiki

http://www.usemod.com/cgi-bin/mb.pl?MeatballWiki

MeatballWiki has been around since 2000 and is one of the longest running wikis. '*Meatball* is a community of active practitioners striving to teach each other how to organise people using online tools. Members here are either community managers or are building supporting tools ... exchanging help when needed, mostly by teaching each other.'[27] Meatball gathers together wiki enthusiasts from around the world, working in several languages, including English, French and German. Because MeatballWiki was established with the goal of exploring collaboration media, it includes some useful advice about how to establish and manage online communities, including the communities that are needed to maintain wikis. Some of its activities, such as an attempt to index all wikis, have not been kept up to date. Others, such as the wiki TourBus[28], a tour of wikis, are updated regularly and provide a good introduction to how public wikis are being used.

Community and interest group wikis

DavisWiki

http://daviswiki.org

The community of Davis, California has developed an extensive, interesting and easy-to-use community information resource in a wiki. It is introduced in this way: 'This project is an interconnected community effort to explore, discuss and compile anything and everything about Davis – especially the little, enjoyable things. This entire site is maintained by the people who use it ...' You must register to edit the wiki, but the process is quick and simple.

Flu Wiki

http://www.fluwikie.com

Flu Wiki was established in mid 2005 in response to the threats posed by avian influenza ('bird flu'). It has grown into a substantial resource covering topics that include the 'basic science' underlying the influenza, epidemiological models, preparedness, national and international plans and surveillance, legal, ethical and economic issues, timeliness, opinions, and rumours. It is possible to join in a discussion forum at the site. This wiki is well laid out and easy to navigate.

PlanetMath

http://planetmath.org

'*PlanetMath* is a virtual community which aims to help make mathematical knowledge more accessible ... the main feature is the mathematics encyclopedia with entries written and reviewed by members.' The site also contains articles and mathematical expositions and links to books and other published materials.

ukcider

http://ukcider.co.uk/wiki

This well-tended site provides an excellent example of how a wiki can be used to develop an information resource in a specific subject area. The wiki provides information about real cider and supports advocacy for real cider enthusiasts and small producers in the UK. It is comprehensive, well laid out, informative and interesting. There are guides to over 500 cider pubs in the UK, producers to visit, upcoming events, retailers and wholesalers, as well as information about French cider makers and how to find cider in France and Spain. There are also recipes for cooking with cider and information about cider making, including fruit, presses, nurseries and pests. Andy Roberts, who established the ukcider wiki, has written an account of his experiences.[29]

DoWire's E-Democracy Best Practices Wiki

http://dowire.org/wiki

Democracy Online Newswire (DoWire) is a website concerned with democracy and the Internet ('e-democracy'). The site includes a wiki which is used as a 'collaborative drafting environment'.[30] The wiki includes, among many other things, a framework for best practices in e-democracy, case studies, conference information and reports and areas for discussion of technologies. Not all pages in this wiki are editable. For example, the pages describing the wiki and its use are locked and pages describing response to the July 2005 London bombings are frozen.

Memory Alpha

http://memory-alpha.org/en/wiki

Memory Alpha is a large and lively reference tool based on the *Star Trek* television and movie series. The wiki is presented as a thematic encyclopaedia with sections for episodes and movies, people, science and technology, society and culture, the universe and more. There are editions in

English, German, French, Dutch and Swedish. A formidable site, spoiled for your reviewer only by a black background which, while atmospheric, is tiring on the eyes.

The Tolkien Wiki Community

http://thetolkienwiki.org

This is another large and popular wiki, for fans of the works of J.R.R. Tolkien.

Information technology wikis

This is a large category of wikis. The information technology community was the earliest user of wikis and many mature wikis have emerged from their experiments with the format. Wikis are used by the information technology research community to share information and by the developers of information systems (both open source and proprietary) to provide product support and documentation.

HDoIP Wiki

http://hdwiki.i2cat.net

This wiki is a reference guide for High Definition over Internet Protocol (HDoIP) and high quality video. It was established by the i2CAT Foundation,[31] in response to initiatives in this field by the Trans-European Research and Education Networking Association (TERENA). Its purpose is to inform international research communities about HDoIP and to involve them, through provision of news and know-how.

Access Grid Wiki

http://www-unix.mcs.anl.gov/fl/research/accessgrid/wiki/moin.cgi

The Access Grid is a set of Internet-based resources that support high-quality, large-format display videoconferencing and other distributed collaborative work. The wiki contains a directory of locations connected to the Access Grid and gathers together information to help resolve the technical issues that arise in this complex environment.

Audacity Wiki

http://www.audacityteam.org/wiki

A good example of a product support wiki is the Audacity audio editor and recorder wiki. Audacity is open source software for fast multi-track recording and editing in a number of digital formats. The software is developed by a community of volunteers. The volunteer developers and the users of Audacity use the wiki to contribute to product documentation, notes and discussion.

Citing wikis

How do you cite a reference to a wiki or wiki page? As with any new publication medium, it takes some time for a standard format of citation to develop, be refined and be accepted. Wiki pages can be cited in similar ways to web pages and, where appropriate, entries in reference works. The major issues for citing wikis centre on authorship and dates. We suggest some resolutions to these issues here.

Because wikis have multiple authors and the authors are often unknown, it is rarely possible to credit authorship of a wiki to a person or group of individuals. Because the authors of a wiki tend to reflect or form a community, we believe that the community can be recognised as an author. Thus, the author of an entry in Wikipedia would be 'Wikipedia' the name representing the community of authors.

When a wiki is used as a source of information, it is important to cite the version of the wiki from which the information has been taken as precisely as possible. Because wiki pages can change frequently, even several times a day, identification of the version of the page from which information has been taken involves citing the time (if it is available) as well as the day, month and year of the revision. Some wikis provide revision numbers, which can be used in place of the time of the revision. Most wikis provide time and date information on each page, but in some wikis you will need to go to the history or revisions page to get this information. Wikis that include the revision number usually include it on either the wiki page itself or the revisions page. Some wikis do not provide date, time and revision information; the most accurate available citation of those wikis would include the time as well as the date that the page was consulted.

A reference to the 'social software' entry in Wikipedia applying these rules and using APA format would appear as:

> Wikipedia. (2006, March 3, 01:49). *Social Software*. Retrieved 4 March, 2006, from http://en.wikipedia .org/wiki/Social_software.

Using Chicago rules, the same citation would appear as:

> Wikipedia. *Social Software* [Wiki]. 01:49, 3 March, 2006 [cited 4 March 2006]. Available from http://en.wikipedia.org/wiki/Social_software.

Notes

1. The 'many eyeballs' maxim is credited to Eric Raymond who described how testers as well as developers can contribute to the identification of software bugs: Raymond, E. S. (2001) 'The cathedral and the bazaar. Musings on Linux and open source by an accidental revolutionary: O'Reilly', pre-publication version available at: *http://www.catb.org/~esr/writings/cathedral-bazaar/cathedral-bazaar* (accessed: 13 January 2006).

2. A web bot is a software program that is written to take certain actions on the World Wide Web ('bot' comes from 'robot'). Benign robots called spiders or crawlers are used to gather the data the search engines index. Internet spammers and vandals may use bots to send spam to multiple e-mail addresses or to add unwanted text to multiple websites, notably wikis.

3. WikiWikiWeb (2006) 'Front page'; available at: *http://www.c2.com/cgi/wiki* (page dated 25 January 2006; accessed: 30 January 2006).

4. Clyde, L. A. (2004) *Weblogs and Libraries*. Oxford: Chandos Publishing.

5. Wikimedia Foundation (2006) 'Home'; available at: *http://wikimediafoundation.org/wiki/Home* (page dated 11:13, 5 January 2006; accessed: 10 January 2006).

6. See: *http://www.wikiquote.org*.

7. See: *http://species.wikipedia.org/wiki/Main_Page*.

8. For an extensive description of Wikipedia, see McKiernan, G. (2005) 'Wikimedia Worlds Part I: Wikipedia', *Library Hi Tech News* 8: 46–54.

9. In December 2005, Wikipedia changed their policy to require registration for the creation of a new article. It was still possible to openly edit Wikipedia entries in January 2006.

10. Wikipedia (2005) 'Wikipedia: text of the GNU Free Documentation License', Version 1.2, November 2002; available at: *http://en.wikipedia.org/wiki/Wikipedia:Text_of_the_GNU_Free_Documentation_License* (page dated 04:16, 6 November 2005; accessed: 13 January 2006).

11. Wikipedia (2006) 'Wikipedia: multilingual statistics'; available at: *http://en.wikipedia.org/wiki/Wikipedia:Multilingual_ statistics* (page dated 22:42, 4 January 2006 (accessed: 13 January 2006).

12. According to *http://www.wikipedia.org* at 13 January 2006.

13. Johnson, G. (2006) 'The nitpicking of the masses vs the authority of the experts', *The New York Times*; available at: *http://www.nytimes.com/2006/2001/2003/science/2003comm .html* (accessed: 13 January 2006). This article points out that the Wikipedia article on the disgraced South Korean stem cell researcher, Hwang Woo Suk, was updated soon after his research was discredited while *Britannica* remained unchanged.

14. Wikipedia (2005) 'Neutral point of view'; available at: *http://en.wikipedia.org/wiki/NPOV* (page dated 20:45, 13 December 2005; accessed: 7 January 2006).

15. Wikinfo (2005) 'Wikinfo: policy/point of view; available at: *http://www.internet-encyclopedia.org/wiki.php?title=Wikinfo: Policy/Point_of_View* (page dated 03:26, 17 April 2005 (accessed: 13 January 2006).

16. Digital Universe, 'The digital universe'; available at: *http://www.digitaluniverse.net/understand/du* (accessed: 7 January 2006.

17. Summary drawn from the Digital Universe website; available at: *http://www.digitaluniverse.net* (accessed: 7 January 2006) and Terdiman (2005) op. cit.

18. See: *http://openguides.org*.

19. Open Guide to London, 'Grubstreet'; available at: *http://london.openguides.org/index.cgi?Grubstreet* (page dated 09:35:29 10 December 2003; accessed: 17 January 2006).

20. CFDL.org (2006) 'Main page'; available at: *http://www.cpdl .org/wiki* (page dated 20:08, 29 January 2006; accessed: 19 January 2006).

21. Wikisource (2006) 'Main page'; available at: *http:// en.wikisource.org/wiki/Main_Page* (page dated 09:50, 8 January 2006; accessed: 29 January 2006).

22. Wikibooks (2006) 'GNU Free Documentation License'; available at: *http://en.wikibooks.org/wiki/GNU_Free_ Documentation_License* (page dated 22:07, 9 January 2006; accessed: 30 January 2006).

23. RadioReference.com, 'RadioReference.com: your complete reference source'; available at: *http://www.radioreference.com* (undated page; accessed: 23 November 2005).

24. Terdiman, D. (2005) 'How wikis are changing our view of the world', *CNET News.com*; available at: *http://news.com.com/Wikis+allow+news,+history+by+committee/2009-1025_3-5944453.html* (accessed: 18 February 2006).

25. Tracking the changes in news content is a little slow because many of the changes are simple style edits.

26. See: *http://www.c2.com/cgi/wiki?StartingPoints* (accessed: 7 January 2006).

27. Meatball (2006) 'MeatballWiki'; available at: *http://www.usemod.com/cgi-bin/mb.pl?MeatballWiki* (page dated 04:17, 30 January 2006; accessed: 30 January 2006).

28. Meatball (2005) 'TourBus'; available at: *http://www.usemod.com/cgi-bin/mb.pl?TourBus* (page dated 09:18, 20 November 2005; accessed: 30 January 2006). See Chapter 3 for more information.

29. Roberts, A. (2005) 'Introducing a WIKI to a community of practice'; available at: *http://www.frankieroberto.com/dad/ultrastudents/andyroberts/year2/AEreport/AEtool.html* (accessed: 9 January 2006).

30. DoWire.org. 'DoWire Wiki'; available at: *http://dowire.org/wiki/Main_Page* (undated page; accessed: 23 November 2005).

31. See: *http://www.i2cat.net/i2cat/servlet/I2CAT.MainServlet?seccio=3.*

3

Wiki finding tools and techniques

Jane Klobas

This chapter introduces tools and techniques for finding wikis and wiki content. Tools for finding wiki hosting services and wiki engines are described in Chapter 7.

There are a number of tools for finding wikis and wiki resources, but the best approach to take depends on what you are looking for and why. People might search for a wiki out of curiosity, to see what wikis look like and what they might contain, or to identify a wiki that might contain specialist information or represent a community to join. There are a number of tools available if you are interested in browsing wikis, but fewer tools for locating specific wikis or searching specifically for information contained in wikis. This chapter begins with a general discussion of the role of Internet search engines in finding wikis and wiki content, then introduces the main tools available for finding and browsing wikis on a specific topic. It concludes with a review of developments in wiki search engines.

Using Internet search engines to find wikis and wiki content

At the time of writing, the wiki community was still developing finding tools for wikis and wiki content. Although several tools show promise, they do not yet offer comprehensive coverage of the wiki universe. Although we recommend that you start your search for a wiki or wiki content with one of the resources specifically designed for wikis, there may still be occasions when you need, or want, to use an Internet search engine. Three problems, however, restrict ability to find wikis or wiki content using generic search engines: limited metadata, indexing delays and in some cases, closure to automatic indexing. This section explains why these problems restrict ability to isolate wikis and wiki content in a generic search engine and suggests some techniques that may be used to limit searches to wikis.

Wikis are not easily identifiable by metadata.[1] Very few wiki engines provide utilities that encourage the creators of wikis or wiki pages to add metadata, and none of the metadata schemes make specific reference to how a web resource might be identified as a wiki. Wikis most often declare themselves to be wikis within the text of the front page, or occasionally, within the title. This limits ability to restrict a search specifically to wikis. For example, adding the word 'wiki' to a search will often retrieve links to web pages that contain the word 'wiki' as well as wikis and wiki pages. Very often, the first pages listed in the search results will refer to Wikipedia.

Given the limited amount of metadata available for searching for wikis, the most effective technique for finding wikis using a search engine relies on the only metadata likely to identify a wiki: the title. Find out how your favourite search engine tags the title field and search for the word 'wiki' in the title. Using Google, for example, you would search for '[search term(s)] intitle:wiki', thus 'learning intitle:wiki' would search for pages that contain the word 'learning' and have the word 'wiki' in the title. Although this strategy is useful, it is imperfect. There is no guarantee that a page with 'wiki' in the title is a wiki rather than a page about a wiki and, of course, this strategy cannot identify a wiki that does not include 'wiki' in the title.

Indexing delays arise because searches on Internet search engines rely on indexes to the Web. These indexes can be 1–2 weeks older than the current content of a site, so if a wiki page has been changed since the index was created, new content is not immediately findable. Or, conversely, the indexed content may no longer be the current content. Furthermore, the algorithms used by search engines to sort sites often rely on links to a site, and there may be delays in the appearance of a new wiki or wiki page near enough to the top of a list of search results to be identifiable. New wikis can therefore take time to emerge as searchable web resources if specific strategies are not taken to identify them as wikis and register them in a directory of wikis.

Search engine indexes are created by bots that automatically search the Web. Unfortunately, spam bots use techniques similar to those used by search engine bots. A wiki that is open to automatic indexing may therefore also be open to spam attacks. While some wiki administrators have dealt with this threat by requiring authors to register before editing a wiki, others opposed to registration have prevented bots from accessing the wiki. This technique can also restrict search engine access, however, and affected wikis are simply not searchable from an Internet search engine. For example, indexing of WorldWideWiki was blocked in 2005 to prevent spam attacks and its content is no longer searchable except from within the wiki itself.[2]

Finding wikis

Finding a wiki may involve use of Internet search engines, directories, and tours and networks. The best places to start browsing for wikis are the directories or tours developed specifically for wikis. Locating a wiki in a specific field is more difficult and may require a combination of consulting wiki directories and tours, and using a generic Internet search engine.

Directories

Several efforts have been made to create directories of wikis. The most comprehensive directories are themselves wikis; members of wiki communities add and maintain details of their own wikis. Some directories attempt to list all wikis, while others are limited to wikis that use a specific search engine or are hosted by a specific wiki hosting service. None of the directories provides a complete list of wikis, so a search for a wiki in a specific area of interest is likely to require a search of several directories.

Wiki Index

http://www.wikiindex.com

Wiki Index, perhaps the most comprehensive directory of wikis, describes itself as a 'wiki of wikis'. It is well structured, with an appealing layout. Each indexed wiki is described in terms of its main topic (chosen from a list provided on the front page of Wiki Index), the wiki engine used, the language or languages of the wiki's contents, its edit mode (from open edit to private) and its status (choices are: vibrant, active, needs love, inactive, goal reached and private). The front page of Wiki Index (see Figure 3.1) allows a user to select a list of wikis in any of the defined categories. The lists themselves are in alphabetical order. Entries for individual wikis can include additional categories as well as the standard information. It is possible to search

Figure 3.1   Wiki Index

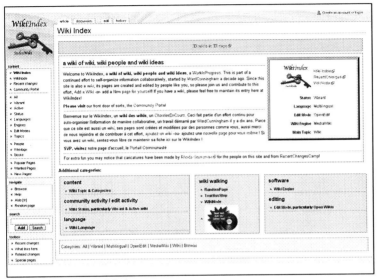

Source: *http://www.wikiindex.com*

the full text of Wiki Index, so all information, including the additional categories, is searchable. Because Wiki Index is itself a wiki, the entry for each indexed wiki can be added and maintained by the community responsible for that wiki.

SwitchWiki

http://www.worldwidewiki.net/wiki/SwitchWiki

SwitchWiki attempts to list all wikis that are publicly available on the Web. It is itself a wiki, so entries can be added and maintained by the community responsible for each included wiki. The wikis are listed in alphabetical order. Although SwitchWiki encourages those registering a wiki to add a description page containing summary information about the wiki along with category tags, this option is not widely used. Consequently, it is not easy to find wikis by subject within SwitchWiki. We expect Wiki Index to overtake SwitchWiki as the most comprehensive wiki index, but SwitchWiki might remain a useful source for information about early wikis.

Public Wiki Forums

http://c2.com/cgi/wiki?PublicWikiForums

This list is hosted on the site of the first wiki, WikiWikiWeb.[3] The directory contained over 250 wikis in December 2005, listed in alphabetical order in each of five categories: computer related (about 110 wikis), not computer related (110), unclassified (22), in German (16), in other languages (11). This directory includes some of the longest running wikis.

Wiki Verzeichnis

http://www.wikiservice.at/gruender/wiki.cgi?WikiVerzeichnis

A German language list of wikis, including wikis in English and German. Some of the wikis are listed by language while others are gathered in broad subject categories.

Blog and Wiki Technology Collaborative Document

http://www.davidmattison.ca/tiki/tiki-index.php?page_ref_id=12

David Mattison maintains a directory of wikis on his site. Although the number of wikis is relatively small, they are well selected for representativeness and quality. A simple and effective classification scheme is used. In December 2005, the categories were: community and general wikis, educational and reference wikis, entertainment and recreational wikis, government wikis, information technology, science and technology wikis, and library and archives wikis. A directory of wiki engines and another of wiki hosting services are also included, along with a short list of readings about wikis.

UseMod Wiki: SiteList

http://www.usemod.com/cgi-bin/wiki.pl?SiteList

This page lists wikis that have been developed using the UseMod wiki engine or close variants of it. Some of the wikis have migrated to other wiki engines since they were originally developed, but remain in the list. Wikis are listed in no particular order and classified using the following headings: public wiki sites (public, edit allowed); websites (public read, private edit); private sites (private and intranet uses); dead links to past wikis. Each wiki is identified by its name and a few words of description, for example, '[BrickWiki], an open-content Lego Wiki'. The language or languages of the wiki text are often included in the description.

Similar sites are maintained for many other wiki engines, including:

- *MoinMoin Wikis* (*http://purl.net/wiki/moin/MoinMoin Wikis*): this directory emphasises the geographical origin and language of the listed wikis;

- *Php Wiki Sites* (*http://phpwiki.sourceforge.net/phpwiki/ PhpWikiSites*): a directory organised by the version of the PHP language in which the listed wiki was written;

- *PmWiki Users* (*http://www.pmwiki.org/wiki/PmWiki/ PmWikiUsers*): categories include commercial sites; education/research; non-profit and other groups; and sites listed by language;

- *TaviSites* (*http://tavi.sourceforge.net/TaviSites*): a list of the known uses of the WikkiTikkiTavi wiki engine;

- *ZwikiSites* (*http://www.zwiki.org/ZwikiSites*): some examples of how the ZWiki engine has been used.

List of Wikia

http://wikia.com/wiki/List_of_Wikia

A list of wikis hosted by the popular Wikia hosting service. Over 700 wikis were included at the end of December 2005. The wikis are listed in alphabetical order in three groups: existing Wikia; popular Wikia; and rejected Wikia. Additional information about each wiki is available by clicking on a link to 'info'. The page 'Category:Wikia descriptions',[4] leads to an alphabetical listing of the tags used to categorise the wikis; wikis using each tag can be found by following the links from the tag. Similarly, wikis can be found by language from the page 'Category:Languages'.[5]

The seedwiki Directory

http://www.seedwiki.com/wiki/seed_wiki/_wiki_directory.cfm

Other hosting services also provide lists of hosted wikis. Most of these are simple alphabetical lists. Unless you know the name of the wiki you are seeking, it is difficult to find a wiki from this type of list, although they can be useful for browsing. An example is the list of wikis hosted by the seedwiki hosting service. Some of the entries in the list are annotated.

Special interest wikis

Some special interest groups are creating directories of wikis in their fields of interest. Public Wiki Forums[6] is useful as a directory of wikis in the computing field. Other directories may be centred on industries, like the example given here.

University-Wikis

http://universitywikinodewiki.wikia.com/wiki/University-wikis

This site has been developed with the aim of listing wikis associated with universities and similar institutions. In late December 2005, it covered German university wikis better than those in other countries. Although the number of wikis included in the site was small (52), several of the sites provide interesting examples of the ways wikis are being used in universities. Another list of wikis in universities and research is available on the PmWiki Users page.[7]

Wiki tours and networks

Wiki TourBus

http://www.usemod.com/cgi-bin/mb.pl?TourBusStop

The wiki TourBus was designed to provide newcomers to wikis – and those who are simply curious about wiki developments – to visit wikis in much the same way you would visit the sights of a city on a tour bus. The site listed here is the wiki tour 'Central Station' at MeatballWiki. From here, or from any other wiki with a wiki 'TourBusStop', you can join a tour of wikis. Tours available at 30 December 2005 were: the Grand Wiki Community Tour, Wiki Developers Tour, Eclectic Wiki Tour, International Wiki Tour, Multilingual Wiki Tour and the UseMod Wiki Tour. Each bus stop includes the name and a brief description of the wiki at the stop, some highlights of the wiki (MeatballWiki also provides a link to the wiki's 'Famous sites') and a link to the next wiki in the tour. It is possible to idle away several hours on a wiki tour.

WikiNode

http://www.worldwidewiki.net/wiki/WikiNode

While the Wiki TourBus provides an interlinked series of wikis to visit, the WikiNode project aims to provide access to a network of wikis. Each participating wiki includes a WikiNode page. The page contains information about the originating wiki and links to other wikis that are likely to be of interest to visitors.

Finding wiki content

To find wiki content, you may need to use a variety of techniques. Although some wiki search engines exist, they only provide access to a limited subset of wikis. We review each of these wiki search engines below. If none of the wiki search engines is suitable for your needs, two additional approaches are available. Public wiki content is searchable using Internet search engines, subject to the (not insubstantial) limitations introduced at the beginning of this chapter. Finally, you can locate a wiki that is likely to contain the information that you are looking for and search within that wiki – but searches within many wikis are limited to specific metadata fields (usually the title) so this approach also has its limitations.

Metawiki Search

http://sunir.org/apps/meta.pl

Metawiki Search is a wiki search engine associated with MeatballWiki. It searches the page titles of 'recognised' wikis. The recognised wikis are primarily those created using first generation open source wiki engines or hosted by services developed using these engines. Because searches are limited to page titles, content that is not reflected in the title cannot be found using Metawiki Search.

Wikisearch

www.wikisearch.org

Wikisearch (a service on Angela Beesley's blog) offers searches of several wikis from one page. Each search remains an individual search of a single wiki using that wiki's search engine, so some searches are limited to title search only. The saving, however, is that you can search several wikis from a single page without having to go into each wiki. The searchable wikis include MeatballWiki, C2 (the site that hosts WikiWikiWeb), Crao (a popular wiki with French and other non-English-speaking wiki developers), wikis hosted in the Wikia hosting service (titles only), and Wikipedia and the other wikis administered by the Wikimedia Foundation (mostly titles only).

Wikia search

http://www.wikia.com/wiki/Special:Search

The Wikia hosting service provides the ability to search by title and keyword across wikis hosted by Wikia, Inc.

Qwika

www.qwika.com

Released in a beta version[8] in February 2006, Qwika aims to provide the ability to search 'all sizeable wikis in all sizeable languages, translate them, make them easily findable in the shortest possible time'. In its initial beta version, it searches Wikipedia and Wikitravel in several languages. If this project meets its goal, it will provide a useful and powerful way to search the content of wikis.

Notes

1. Metadata is the data that describes a web page or other electronic information resource. Metadata is recorded in fields. It describes the resource in terms of its primary characteristics. Most web resources, for example, have a title field. Some may have a creator or author field, a date field and fields to describe the subject and format of the resource. A popular metadata scheme is the international standard, Dublin Core; for more information see *http://dublincore.org.*
2. See: *http://www.worldwidewiki.net/wiki/WikiSpam.*
3. See: *http://c2.com/cgi/wiki.*
4. See: *http://wikia.com/wiki/Category:Wikia_descriptions.*
5. See: *http://wikia.com/wiki/Category:Languages.*
6. See: *http://c2.com/cgi/wiki?PublicWikiForums.*
7. See: *http://www.pmwiki.org/wiki/PmWiki/PmWikiUsers.*
8. The beta version of a software or service is a version released to users for testing in a real environment. Once any problems or bugs identified during this period of testing are fixed, the software or service is released in its final, production form.

4

Wikis in library and information science

Jane Klobas and
Kristín Ó Hlynsdóttir

In this chapter, we concentrate on how wikis are being used in the field of library and information science (LIS). As a field concerned with information, LIS has been one of the first fields after computer science to adopt wikis for a range of uses. Many of the contributors to LIS wikis are practitioners, teachers or researchers, and most of them would say that their primary interest and skills are in information rather than technology. LIS therefore provides an example of how wikis might be adopted in a field of study and practice by people who do not necessarily have a technical background. The chapter introduces a collection of wikis used for library work as well as others considered useful for information professionals in LIS and related fields. This is not an exhaustive list of wikis in LIS and, as with the wikis described in other chapters, there may be some changes by the time you read this book. A list of wikis in LIS is maintained by David Mattison on his website.[1]

In preparing this chapter, we asked the readers and contributors to LIS Internet discussion groups why they thought wikis were important for LIS. The majority of responses pointed to the value of wikis for collaboration among geographically dispersed working groups (whether working in the same university or city or across the globe). Others also noted the ease with which readers can become contributors. Jon Haupt of Iowa State University suggested that the value goes beyond the simple creation of shared information resources to sense making: 'wikis represent a new paradigm of information sharing, one of a more dynamic collaborative information gathering system. When people use wikis, they are creating information out of data, making sense of the "stuff" that they are putting in'.[2] Respondents also noted that the LIS community is still experimenting with wikis and we still do not know what forms will emerge as the most common or useful. Several also noted hesitation among members of the community to contribute. A number of possible explanations were provided for this hesitation, including the need for a larger community of contributors prepared to provide examples, modesty about the quality or authority of one's own contributions, fear of one's contributions being criticised by others and lack of familiarity with the ways in which contributions can be made to wikis.

The LIS community began formally discussing the possibilities of using wikis early in 2004. In February, the UK Online User Group[3] (now the UK eInformation Group) held a half-day seminar on blogs and wikis in London. In November 2004, members of the American Society for Information Science and Technology's Special Interest Group on Science and Information Technology systems met at the Society's annual meeting to hear Sunir Shah, the editor of MeatballWiki and Ross Mayfield, CEO of the wiki software company, Socialtext, speak about wikis.[4] More meetings were held in both the UK and North America during 2005. There was a 'Blogs, wikis and collaboration tools' track at the Internet Librarian International conference held in London in October[5] and one of the keynote sessions at the Online Information Conference, again in London in November/December, featured wikis.[6] Members of the LIS community have also contributed to discussions of wikis among members of the wiki community. One of the presentations at the Wikimania conference held in Frankfurt in August 2005 described how German Wikipedia volunteers have matched names in biographies in the German version of Wikipedia to the unique name ID assigned by the German National Library (DDB), thus linking Wikipedia to the DDB catalogue for works on or by the author.[7]

During 2005 and into 2006, the LIS community moved from talking about the possibilities of wikis to training for their development and management. A number of LIS wikis were established during 2005 and the creators of some of these wikis described them to their colleagues in papers and presentations.[8] The potential of wikis in LIS has been noted by several authors in the field, including Meredith Farkas, the founder of the Library Success wiki[9] who said in 2005: 'The possibilities for what libraries can do with wikis are endless. At their least, they are spaces for quick and easy collaborative work. At their best, they can become true community resources that can position the library as an online hub of their local community.'[10] Farkas suggested a number of applications of wikis in libraries. Wikis could be used jointly by librarians and library patrons to create subject guides; both librarians and patrons could add material to a wiki subject guide and keep links up to date, and in addition, librarians could act as moderators who evaluate resources and remove those that do not meet their standards as information resources. Extending this notion, Farkas suggested that libraries could create 'community wikis' in which members of a community record information that is useful for a local community, such as sports schedules and information about restaurants and hard-to-find specialist services. Farkas also described several ways in which librarians could use wikis internally: as a replacement for rounds of group e-mail, to jointly write documents, to keep the intranet and documents, such as procedures and policy manuals, up to date, and as a conference guide to enhance the experience of attending a conference. In the following sections, we will look at what the LIS community has done with these and other types of wiki.

Wikis for information professionals

A number of wikis have been established to support the work of information professionals, including those working in general information management as well as in libraries. These wikis have had varying degrees of success, perhaps based on the breadth of their appeal. We begin our description of LIS wikis with a best practice wiki for libraries, a growing wiki that meets the needs of practising librarians to share their best practices and supporting materials.

Library Success: A Best Practices Wiki

http://www.libsuccess.org

The Library Success wiki is one of the most widely known LIS wikis. It is intended for librarians to share their success stories. Its creator is Meredith Farkas, a distance learning librarian at Norwich University in Northfield, Vermont. The wiki presents practices by category. In January 2006, there were ten major categories covering professional and management issues, library work and technology. Within the major categories, there were 75 subcategories, each corresponding to a wiki page or article. Different categories and pages have attracted differing levels of contribution from members of the Library Success community. The professional category, for example, includes eight articles, such as conferences and continuing education opportunities, which includes links to conferences and blogs and websites to watch. The marketing article in the 'selling your library' category includes marketing tips and success stories. A sample article appears in Figure 4.1. Between its creation in July 2005 and January 2006, this site has attracted around 8,000 hits a month.[11] By January 2006, 80 contributors and users had included their names in the list of members of the Library Success community.

Figure 4.1   **Extract from the Library Success website design page**

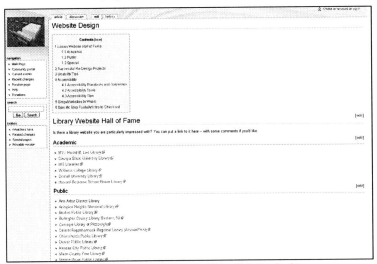

Source: *http://www.libsuccess.org/index.php?title=Website_Design*

LIS Wiki

http://www.liswiki.com

LIS Wiki is a free online LIS encyclopaedia open to contribution by anyone. While Library Success is a collection of best practice descriptions and materials, LIS Wiki was designed to collect and share knowledge in the form of an encyclopaedia. It was launched in June 2005, and by January 2006 there were over 25,000 hits to the main page.[12] There were links to nearly 1,300 articles in 75 categories, the majority of which (94 per cent in a sample of 50 random pages) were stubs containing a basic definition of each topic. The founder of LIS Wiki, John Hubbard, created this wiki with the idea of gathering information that did not meet Wikipedia's criteria for inclusion.[13] In December 2005, Hubbard commented that there was a lot of potential for wikis in LIS, as seen by the number of LIS wikis that have been started. The most difficult issue, though, has been attracting more contributors.[14] It is possible that, as with all wikis, LIS Wiki is being defined over time by its community of users and contributors who see more need for a dictionary than an encyclopaedia.

IAwiki

http://www.iawiki.net/IAwiki

This wiki was created as a 'collaborative knowledge base'[15] for information architecture in spring 2001. It is open for contribution by anyone: no registration is required although visitors are encouraged to sign the IAwiki visitors' book. Rarely a day goes by without a new contribution to this wiki. In December 2005, we asked subscribers to LIS discussion lists to tell us which wikis they thought should be included in this book. IAwiki was among the top three, so it is clearly valued by members of its community. It is, however, a bit daunting for first-time users who are unable to see the wiki's structure or coverage from the front page. The front page directs new users to starting points and 'RoadMaps' which act much like portals for users in different categories. Among the features of the site are a large page dedicated to the ongoing issue of defining information architecture and a list of information architecture blogs and books of interest. There is a site index which, at the beginning of 2006, listed almost 1,000 pages, although some of the pages only contained a link to a page outside the wiki.[16]

CMS Wiki

http://www.cmswiki.com/tiki-index.php

The Content Management Systems (CMS) wiki is a well-established and well-populated knowledge base for content management professionals. The wiki includes definitions and information about events, vendors and consultants (including well-known figures in the field). There is information about CMS newsletters, books, conferences and even jobs in content management.

DigiWik: The Digitization Wiki

http://www.digiwik.org/wiki

How do you go about making digital copies of materials in libraries, museums or even in your home office? DigiWik was launched in 2005 to help individuals and organisations with digitisation needs. It provides definitions, explanations and importantly, links to useful documents. There is also a directory of blogs and newsletters on digitisation. Anyone can contribute to this wiki.

LIANZA IT-SIG Wiki

http://wiki.lianza.org.nz

This wiki is an example of a wiki for a professional association or special interest group. It has been developed by the Information Technology Special Interest Group (ITSIG) of the Library and Information Association of New Zealand Aotearoa (LIANZA). It contains information about the group, a diary of events, a research register (and index to the register) and other resources about the application of information technology to library and information management.

Wikis in LIS education

A number of teachers have experimented with the use of wikis in LIS education. Uses include development of information resources for students, repositories and showplaces of materials, such as essays and portfolios developed by students, collaborative workspaces for group work and workspaces for classroom activities. For example, Susan Maret of the University of Denver has designed a class exercise in which a wiki is used to develop a shared class definition of information secrecy.[17] In this section, we provide an example of an LIS education wiki and refer to a wiki that is being developed as a resource for teachers in LIS.

ZSR Microtext and Government Docs

http://www.seedwiki.com/wiki/zsr_microtext_and_govdocs

Lauren Pressley of Lake Forest University in North Carolina started a wiki for students in the microtext and government

Figure 4.2 Introduction to Lake Forest University's Microtext and Government Documents wiki

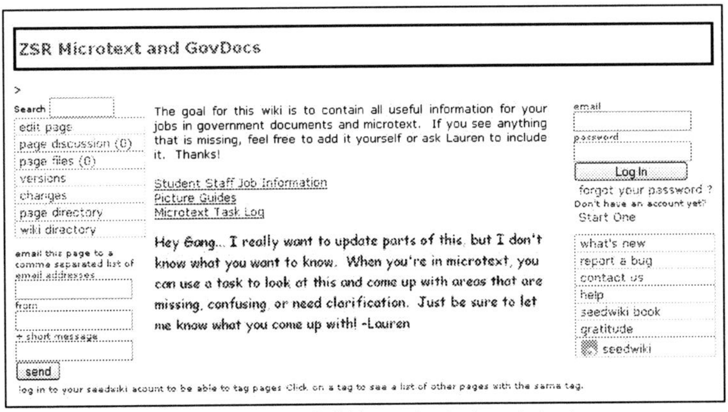

ZSR Microtext and GovDocs

>
Search
edit page
page discussion (0)
page files (0)
versions
changes
page directory
wiki directory

email this page to a
comma separated list of
email addresses

from

+ short message

send

log in to your seedwiki acount to be able to tag pages Click on a tag to see a list of other pages with the same tag.

The goal for this wiki is to contain all useful information for your jobs in government documents and microtext. If you see anything that is missing, feel free to add it yourself or ask Lauren to include it. Thanks!

Student Staff Job Information
Picture Guides
Microtext Task Log

Hey Gang... I really want to update parts of this, but I don't know what you want to know. When you're in microtext, you can use a task to look at this and come up with areas that are missing, confusing, or need clarification. Just be sure to let me know what you come up with! -Lauren

email
password
Log In
forgot your password ?
Don't have an account yet?
Start One

what's new
report a bug
contact us
help
seedwiki book
gratitude
seedwiki

Source: *http://www.seedwiki.com/wiki/zsr_microtext_and_govdocs*

documents departments of her university. The wiki replaced several print and electronic sources of information as well as e-mail updates for non-sensitive information. In addition to consolidating previously dispersed information into a single source, Pressley hopes that in the longer term, students will put more of their own material online rather than relying on her to keep information sources updated.[18] Figure 4.2 gives an idea of the purpose, tone and content of this educational wiki.

Info Teach

http://www.infoteach.org/wiki

Info Teach was established by Chris Powis of Northampton University in the UK as an information resource for teachers in all LIS contexts. His goal is 'to create an online community of practice for librarians and information workers who teach, ... to be international and to cover all sectors [including] reader development, enquiry work, training as well as more traditional group and individual teaching'.[19] As of January 2006, the structure of the wiki was in place and the number of entries was growing, but much was yet to be populated.

Wikis for library instruction

Library instruction is the process of teaching how to use the library. It is a common practice in university libraries where students learn about the resources of a field, how to evaluate them as sources of information, and how to conduct research to identify suitable resources.

Matthies, Helmke and Slater describe the use of the Butler WikiRef wiki[20] in library instruction at Butler University in the USA.[21] Students worked in teams to identify resources in the subject area of interest (business) and to post the resource and an evaluation of it to the appropriate wiki page. The collaborative activity engaged students and teachers much more than the standard lecture-based format for this type of instruction. In addition, it created a repository of student work that could be used by students to compare different teams' results, and by teachers to evaluate student work.

Library Instruction Wiki

http://instructionwiki.org

There is also a wiki about library instruction. The Library Instruction Wiki was set up by the Oregon Library Association's (*http://www.olaweb.org*) Library Instruction Roundtable as a repository for library instruction materials and a more general resource for librarians interested in instruction. Resources available from the site include handouts and tutorials, teaching tips, links to websites created for classes and a (still to be completed) glossary and bibliography. An example is a link to the Boolean Logic QuickTip document contributed by Pierce College. This is not a large wiki, but it is quite frequently accessed (by our estimate, about 1,000 times a month in late 2005/early 2006). Librarians and others interested in instruction are urged to contribute.

The process of setting up the Library Instruction wiki and some of the philosophy behind it, was described by Rachel Bridgewater and Anne-Marie Deitering at the Internet Librarian International conference in London in October 2005.[22] They noted the benefits of using a community-maintained wiki instead of a clearinghouse that relies on staff of a single organisation finding time to add resources and keep links up to date. They also commented on some potential barriers to adoption of the wiki by members of the community and described the actions they took to overcome these barriers, such as making the visual appearance of the wiki attractive to newcomers, establishing a structure that was meaningful to all potential contributors rather than idiosyncratic to the founders of the wiki, and developing resources to help contributors who are not familiar with wiki syntax, culture and structure to feel comfortable adding their contributions.

Conference wikis

Several LIS conferences have experimented with wikis. We have included reviews of a small selection here.

ALA Chicago 2005

http://meredith.wolfwater.com/wiki

Meredith Farkas, the creator of the Library Success wiki created an unofficial wiki for the 2005 American Library

Association (ALA) Annual Conference in Chicago. Her motivation was to draw on the help of the library community to provide advice that would help first-time conference attendees to orient themselves to both Chicago and the conference. The wiki captured the imagination of conference goers who added (among other things) restaurant reviews, useful information about Chicago, such as guides to transport and WiFi, and conference information ranging from official and unofficial lists of conference events to individuals' conference schedules.[23]

ASIST 2005 Annual Meeting Wiki

http://www.ils.unc.edu/asist2005/wiki

A wiki containing similar information was created as the official wiki for the ASIST 2005 annual meeting. Because this wiki was seeded with information before the conference began, it was perhaps less active than the ALA Chicago wiki, but provided a platform for posting documents and links during and after the conference.

Knowledgenetworker Wiki

http://wiki.knowledgenetworker.net

We have included this wiki because it arose from discussions at a conference. It is no longer active (as far as we can tell) but provides a record of several months in the life of a small community of people interested in personal knowledge management between two conferences on the subject. They identify the members of the community, discuss hot topics, such as whether their area of interest should indeed be called personal knowledge management and generally continue and extend for a time, the discussions begun at the conference.

Wikis for co-operative projects and collaborative authoring

Library and information work has long been characterised by cooperation. Wikis have been adopted to support both large-scale international projects and small-scale local projects. Some of the most important organisations in LIS are using wikis for projects, such as development of handbooks and standards. Many of these wikis are private, but some are open for others to view. In this section, we introduce several wikis used in cooperative projects at local, regional and international scale.

OCLC User-contributed Content Pilot

OCLC Research hosts WorldCat, a catalogue of the library holdings of more than 9,000 organisations worldwide.[24] In October 2005, OCLC launched the User-contributed Content Pilot which enables WorldCat contributors to add additional information about their holdings. While not all additional information can be edited by other contributors, wiki functionality allows contributors to add tables of contents and collaboratively author other information, such as notes about the historical context of a work.[25] The wiki engine that enables this functionality is an open source product known as WikiD.[26]

NEMLA Directory of Music Libraries Draft

http://www.seedwiki.com/wiki/nemla_directory_of_music_li braries_draft/nemla_directory_of_music_libraries_draft.cfm

This wiki was used to produce an updated directory of music library collections in the New England region of the USA. It includes information about the libraries, their personnel, opening hours, stacks and more. Although it is no longer maintained, it provides a good example of how a wiki can be used to simplify the collection of data for a shared resource.

OAI Best Practices

http://oai-best.comm.nsdl.org/cgi-bin/wiki.pl?OAI_Best_Practices

This is an example of a wiki established to support to activities of a technical working group. The Open Archives Initiative (OAI) established this wiki as a workspace for individuals and organisations contributing to its Protocol for Metadata Harvesting. Metadata harvesting can be used to build archives of documents drawn from multiple digital libraries and other electronic repositories.[27] The wiki was designed 'to be the staging area for development of documents, etc. for the target audience consisting of OAI data providers, OAI service providers, metadata creators, etc.'[28] and contains several types of documents.

colLib

http://collib.info

colLib is a 'collaborative platform for organising open access materials in Library & Information Science'.[29] This wiki was created in the summer of 2005 by Magnus Enger, a Masters student of Science of Documentation at the University of Tromsø, Norway 'as an experiment in order to explore whether documents in Open Archives Initiative Protocol for Metadata Harvesting-compliant repositories can be organised by end users'.[30] Anyone can contribute to this wiki by adding a category tag to a document that has been gathered from one of the harvested repositories.

(For an article to appear in colLib, it must first be entered in one of the repositories.) Enger measures the success of the wiki by looking at the increase in tagged records over time, his ability to fight spam, as well as the amount of positive feedback. By December 2005, 16 per cent of the 4,389 records were tagged and six spammers had been blocked. Enger blogs about the developments of colLib at *http://collib.blogspot.com.* As a student project wiki, it will only be online until the summer of 2007 unless another means is found to maintain it.

Library wikis

Libraries are using wikis to provide information and services to their patrons and to host staff information. A range of examples is provided here.

Wikis for library patrons

Libraries have taken different approaches to development of wikis for library patrons. Some libraries restrict wiki contributions to staff while others permit patrons to contribute to some pages.

Ohio University Libraries Biz Wiki

http://www.library.ohiou.edu/subjects/bizwiki/

The Biz Wiki is a guide to the business information resources available through Ohio University Libraries. It was developed in MediaWiki so has the familiar structure of Wikipedia. Links from each entry take the user to the resource or to the library catalogue from which members of the university community can access the resource.

Butler WikiRef

http://www.seedwiki.com/wiki/butler_wikiref

The reference wiki of Butler University Libraries, Indiana is 'a collaborative review of databases, books, websites, etc., that are part of the collection of Reference Resources available at or via the Butler University Libraries'. The goal is for the wiki to function 'like a Reference User's Group that facilitates discussion between and the empowering of reference users.'[31] Butler librarians, faculty and students are encouraged to add reference materials that they have used in their university activities, as well as comments about the usefulness of reference materials in general or for specific classes. This wiki has been created using the seedwiki engine. Resource descriptions are accessible as links from a single list in alphabetical order, but there are no links to the resources themselves.

SJCPL's Subject Guides

http://www.libraryforlife.org/subjectguides/index.php/ Main_Page

St. Joseph County Public Library in Indiana has begun to build its subject guides in wiki format. Only librarians have permission to edit them.

Shields Library

http://daviswiki.org/Shields_Library

Among the wikis hosted by the Community of Davis, California,[32] is an editable page about the Shields Library, the third largest library in the University of California system. The page presents the library in an attractive and welcoming light to members of the wider community. Registered users of the DavisWiki can edit this page.

SPSU Wiki

http://wiki.spsu.edu

The Southern Polytechnic State University in Georgia has established a wiki that aims to improve communication and develop community among students, faculty, staff and friends of the university by recording information, 'thoughts and memories'.[33] Much of the material in this wiki is about the university library and its archives and special collections.

LibWiki

http://wiki.uwinnipeg.ca

At the University of Winnipeg in Canada, the Library has joined with the Technology Solutions Centre and other university staff to develop a wiki designed 'to help University of Winnipeg students use technology productively, whether that means walking into the Library and finding a few scholarly sources for an assignment, using your laptop to write a paper, or finding a lab on campus that has SPSS'.[34] The wiki contains information that is useful for teachers as well as students.

LITS

http://wiki.library.vanderbilt.edu/lits/

Library Information Technology Services (LITS) staff at the Jean and Alexander Heard Library at Vanderbilt University in Nashville use a wiki to disseminate information about library technology to library patrons. The site includes information about the status of the library's online catalogue, guidelines for secure computing and LITS reports.

Wikis for library staff

Apart from using wikis to construct resources for library patrons, librarians are using wikis to support their own work.

University of Minnesota Libraries Staff Website

http://wiki.lib.umn.edu

The University of Minnesota Libraries intranet is a wiki. The site contains official information for library staff, ranging from organisational structure (which is, innovatively, summarised in a clickable organisation chart on the homepage) to the university travel policy. Staff are encouraged to contribute.

Karl E. Mundt Library, Dakota State University

The Karl E. Mundt Library at Dakota State University is using a wiki to improve communication among staff. The pages include: out of the office, student workers, projects for student workers and current reference questions. Most of the eight library staff are using the wiki. To introduce the wiki, Todd Quinn, the instruction/reference librarian gave his colleagues a 30-minute demonstration.[35] Figure 4.3 shows a sample page from the wiki.

Miami University Libraries

Rob Withers (2005) describes the wiki used by information desk staff at Miami University.[36] Because the information

Figure 4.3 Sample current research questions page from the Karl E. Mundt Library staff wiki

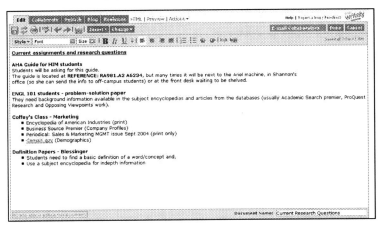

desk is operated by different staff at different times, techniques are needed to share information about the status of library equipment and answers to common enquiries. Libraries typically use logs (either printed or on electronic discussion lists) or paper notes to share this type of information. At Miami University, a wiki has replaced these other forms. The wiki, which has been operating since 2004, contains some information that is relatively static, such as library facilities, services and hours, basic information about reference interview techniques, clock-in/clock-out procedures for staff and renovation updates. The main section of the wiki, however, reflects the queries that are posed at the desk. Withers describes entries that 'include information about a heavily used service that crashed frequently during final exam week, a business research question that can be answered only by using a product available on one machine in the reference area, and troubleshooting networking problems'.[37] Advantages of this system include that it can be accessed by staff at any location, there is no need for a 'gatekeeper' to post information or approve it, information is not lost as it might be when a blog entry is edited and staff do not have to search for information as they do in a log kept in an electronic discussion list.

Quest Wiki (University of Connecticut Libraries)

http://wiki.lib.uconn.edu/wiki/QUEST_Main_Page

The University of Connecticut Libraries created a wiki for information and discussion about the library's catalogue system. All but the proprietary information on this page can be read by visitors. This wiki is being replaced with user guides, but the main page of the QUEST wiki looks quite different from other LIS wikis and is worth a visit.

NSDL Evaluation Wiki

http://eval.comm.nsdlib.org/cgi-bin/wiki.pl?THE_NSDL_EVALUATION_WIKI

The National Science Digital Library (NSDL) was established in the USA in 2000 by the National Science Foundation (NSF) 'to create, develop and sustain a national digital library supporting science, technology, engineering and mathematics (STEM) education.' The NSDL Core Integration group created a wiki to support their evaluation of the NSDL and related projects preparatory to presenting a report to the NSF by the end of 2006. 'The NSDL Evaluation Wiki will archive important documents related to the evaluation process, including the background documents that inform the evaluation process, examples of surveys and questionnaires, preliminary evaluation results, and links to online research related to digital library use and evaluation.'[38]

Notes

1. Mattison, D. (2006) 'Library and archives wikis'; available at: *http://www.davidmattison.ca/tiki/tiki-index.php?page_ ref_id=38* (page dated 07:31:37, 11 January, 2006; accessed: 7 February 2006).
2. Haupt, J. (2005) Personal communication.
3. See: *www.ukolug.org.*
4. ASIST (2004) 'Beyond the sandbox: Wikis and blogs that get work done (SIG STI)'. Abstract of session held at ASIST 2004 Annual Meeting, Managing and Enhancing Information: Cultures and Conflicts (ASIST AM 04), Providence, Rhode Island, 13–18 November 2004; available at:*http://www.asis.org/ Conferences/AM04/abstracts/114.html* (accessed 23 March 2006).
5. See: *http://www.internet-librarian.com/2005Presentations/.*
6. See: *http://www.online-information.co.uk/ol05/day2overview .html.*
7. Voss, J. (2005) 'Metadata with Peronendaten and beyond'. Paper presented at the Wikimania conference, Frankfurt, Germany, 4–8 August 2005; available at: *http://en.wikibooks.org/ w/index.php?title=Wikimania05/JV2* (accessed: 7 February 2006).
8. See, for example, Bridgewater, R. and Deitering, A.-M. (2005) 'Collaborating with wikis'. Paper presented at the Internet Librarian International 2005, London, 10–11 October 2005; available at: *http://www.vancouver.wsu.edu/fac/bridgewa/ili/* (accessed: 7 February 2006); Frumkin, J. (2005) 'Digital libraries: Modern practices, future visions', OCLC *Systems and Services* 21(1): 18–22; Hubbard, J. (2005) 'Liswiki: the first 30 days', *Ex Libris* 257 (July); available at: *http:// marylaine.com/exlibris/xlib257.html* (accessed: 21 October 2005); Kelly, B. (2005) 'Web focus: experiences of using a wiki for note-taking at a workshop', *Ariadne* 42 (January); available at: *http://www.ariadne.ac.uk/issue42/web-focus*; and papers presented at Computers & Libraries 2006; available at: *http://www.infotoday.com/cil2006/wednesday .shtml#TrackC*, forthcoming.
9. See: *http://www.libsuccess.org.*

10. Farkas, M. (2005) 'Using wikis to create online communities', *WebJunction*; available at: *http://webjunction.org/do/DisplayContent?id=11264* (accessed: 6 February 2006).

11. Library Success (2006) 'Main page'; available at: *http://www.libsuccess.org* (page dated 21:09, 28 January 2006; accessed: 9 February 2006).

12. LIS Wiki (2006) 'Main page'; available at: *http://www.liswiki.com* (page dated 13:08, 23 January 2006; accessed: 9 February 2006).

13. Hubbard, op. cit; LIS Wiki (2006) 'LISWiki: About'; available at: *http:www.liswiki.com/wiki/LISWiki:About* (page dated 20:11, 5 February 2006; accessed: 10 February 2006).

14. Hubbard, J. (2005) Personal communication.

15. IAwiki (2005) 'IAWiki'; available at: *http://www.iawiki.net/IAwiki* (page dated 15:44, 31 October 2005; accessed: 10 February 2006).

16. IAwiki (2006) 'List of all pages'; available at: *http://www.iawiki.net/cgi-bin/wiki.pl?action=index* (page dated 16:07, 9 February 2006; accessed: 10 February 2006).

17. Maret, S. (2005) Personal communication.

18. Pressley, L. (2005) Personal communication.

19. Powis, C. (2005) Personal communication.

20. See: *http://www.seedwiki.com/wiki/butler_wikiref*.

21. Matthies, B., Helmke, J. and Slater, P. (2006) 'Using a wiki to enhance library instruction' *Indiana Libraries* 25(3): in press.

22. Bridgewater and Deitering, op. cit.

23. Farkas, op. cit.

24. OCLC, 'WorldCat'; available at: *http://www.oclc.org/worldcat* (accessed: 10 February 2006).

25. OCLC, 'User-contributed Content Pilot'; available at: *http://www.oclc.org/worldcat/open/usercontent* (accessed: 10 February 2006).

26. OCLC Research, 'WikiD'; available at: *http://alcme.oclc.org/wikid* (accessed: 10 February 2006).

27. For an explanation of metadata harvesting and more information about the OAI, see the Wikipedia definition at: *http://en.wikipedia.org/wiki/Open_Archives_Initiative_Protocol_for_Metadata_Harvesting* (page dated 06:04, 5 February 2006; accessed: 10 February 2006).

28. Digital Library Federation and NSDL OAI and Shareable Metadata Best Practices Working Group (2006) 'OAI best practices'; available at: *http://oai-best.comm.nsdl.org/cgi-bin/wiki.pl?OAI_Best_Practices* (page dated 13:06, 13 October 2006; accessed: 10 February 2006).

29. ColLib (2006) 'Main page'; available at: *http://collib.info* (page dated 10:08, 3 January 2006; accessed: 12 February 2006).

30. ColLib (2005) 'ColLib: About'; available at: *http://collib.info/index.php?title=ColLib:About* (page dated 13:44, 26 August 2005 (accessed: 12 February 2006).

31. Butler WikiRef, 'Home Page'; available at: *http://www.seedwiki.com/wiki/butler_wikiref* (page dated 04:35:33, 8 June 2005]; accessed: 7 February 2006).

32. See: *http://daviswiki.org.*

33. SPSU Wiki (2005) 'SPSU Wiki:About'; available at: *http://wiki.spsu.edu/index.php/SPSU_Wiki:About* (page dated 02:05, 28 August 2005; accessed: 11 February 2006).

34. LibWiki, University of Winnipeg (2006) 'Main Page'; available at: *http://www.uwinnipeg.ca* (page dated 04:01, 11 February 2006; accessed: 11 February 2006).

35. Quinn, T. (2005) personal communication.

36. Withers, R. (2005) 'Something wiki this way comes: An interactive way of posting, updating and tracking changes in information used by library staff', *College & Research Libraries News* 66(11): 775–7.

37. Ibid., p. 776.

38. Information taken from NSDL Evaluation Wiki. *NSDL Evaluation Wiki Home*; available at: *http://eval.comm.nsdlib.org/cgi-bin/wiki.pl?THE_NSDL_EVALUATION_WIKI* (page dated 10:59, 18 January 2006; accessed: 11 February 2006).

5

Wikis in business
Sébastien Paquet

This chapter provides an overview of business uses of wikis. The combination of simplicity, transparency and openness that wikis offer is an excellent response to the needs of today's dynamic, collaborative, knowledge-intensive work environments. Because wikis are a very flexible communication medium, the chapter cannot offer a comprehensive list of actual and potential uses. Nevertheless, the explanations and examples given will convey the general flavour of what has been done with wikis in corporate environments and give a glimpse of the possibilities.

The chapter begins with a look at those characteristics of wikis that distinguish them from other types of collaboration software or groupware used in business organisations. We then present a picture of wiki use within organisations, both at the general level, and with more detail using a few examples. Finally, we analyse three prominent patterns of wiki use in businesses: as a tool for project and group collaboration, as a knowledge base and as a means of gathering and disseminating new information internally.

How are wikis different?

> The key is that the workspace did not impose the processes. (Aaron Burcell, VP Marketing, Stata Labs)[1]

What makes wikis different from other intranet or collaboration software (i.e. applications that enable network users to interact or work together) in common use in business?

- *Unconstrained structure.* Content in wikis is not required to follow any prescribed structure. In that respect, wikis work differently from more structured forms of communication, such as project management software featuring predefined fields for users to fill in. As a medium, wikis encourage creative manipulation and do not constrain communication.[2] Their flexibility may be perceived as a lack of sophistication, but this is what actually enables them to serve many different functions.

- *Supports informal communication.* Wikis accommodate a range of formality in communication. Because content in a wiki is free-form, wikis make it especially easy to freely exchange ideas, for example, letting users annotate and comment in a personal voice when and where needed without feeling out of place.

- *Simplicity.* Wikis are simple and easy to learn. Little to no knowledge of markup or code is necessary to be able to use them productively. From a technical standpoint there is little to distinguish expert users from novices. The low barrier to contribution fosters adoption. The powerful feeling of creating their own web of information seduces users; the ease of understanding how a wiki works seduces managers.

- *Content is king.* Wikis eschew fancy appearance. Most wikis purposefully leave little room to fiddle with layout, colours and such, unlike a word processor or presentation software. What formatting options are available are there to help structure the content. Wikis thus drive users to concentrate on content and structure.

- *Links rule.* Wikis were designed as an environment that makes linking easy, opening up the possibilities that hypertext affords to structure information.

- *Open, flat hierarchy.* Few wikis implement a hierarchy among users and a permission structure, as is often present in other enterprise software. Where there is a permission structure, it is usually very flat and open – for example, only the administrators of a given wiki will be able to invite new users in. Otherwise, once you are in the wiki, every page can be read and edited.

Organisations that use wikis

Since their inception ten years ago, wikis have progressively spread from the core software development environment where they were born, out to the thousands of websites we see on the Web today, in an increasingly wide array of work contexts, and to an unknown, but significant, number of internal sites not seen on the Web. With so much of work having become knowledge- and information-driven, the need to share and collaborate has become manifest in many sectors; this trend, together with the explosive popularity and availability of Web-based technology, has fuelled the adoption of wikis.

Wikis have come to be used in a multitude of business settings, from small firms all the way up to very large enterprises. By and large, these wikis are behind a corporate firewall or are password-protected, making research data harder to obtain and their exploration and analysis more difficult than public wikis. A few surveys and case studies have been conducted to probe into wiki use.

The Gilbane Report, a content management technology newsletter, surveyed its readers in 2005 and found that a majority of the 91 respondents used wiki or blog technology. The leading applications were knowledge management, internal information dissemination and project communication.[3]

Peter Thoeny and Dan Woods conducted a number of interviews with corporate wiki key users and experts in preparation for their book *Wikis in the Workplace: A Practical Guide to Collaborating, Creating Knowledge and Sharing Information.*[4] They found that in some companies, wikis had already moved from being a marginal or experimental technology to being a support for mission critical information. Thoeny and Woods also learned that larger enterprises may have up to dozens of independent wikis. Indeed, some enterprises are at a stage where they envision consolidating decentralised wikis into a central system, maintained by the IT department.

Here we briefly describe three specific examples of corporate use of wiki technology, providing references to published case studies featuring more detail.

Ziff Davis Media

1UP.com is the gaming division of Ziff Davis Media, one of the largest technology magazine publishers in the USA. The new general manager Tom Jessiman had noticed 'a lot of confusion using e-mail, well over 100 group e-mails a day, which was unwieldy, even nightmarish. Nobody knew which was the latest version of an attachment, everything was lost in inboxes and you had to data-mine your e-mails to find anything.'[5] He sought an efficient and effective alternative to e-mail and attachments as a way of working together. His group started using a Socialtext wiki in 2003.

The initial use was as a strategic planning tool. Upon the general manager's direction, the editorial team used the wiki to brainstorm ideas for future articles and determine an editorial calendar. Later, the heads of the departments in charge of putting stories together realised they could use Socialtext for day-to-day coordination, scheduling and requests. The groups need to communicate to each other what is needed for stories in progress, such as art, HTML requests and copy, all in a back-and-forth conversational style. The groups set up a page for each activity, posting requests as they come up and tracking fulfilment of the request. The ability of the tool to support informal communication was key in supporting a process that frequently encounters exceptions that have to be cleared up. Moreover, the transparency of the tool helped other departments, such as marketing, be aware of what they would be selling.

Wikis were rapidly adopted for other ends. They enabled the team developing a new version of the 1UP.com website (which included three external vendors) to brainstorm ideas for the new site and to post and annotate specifications and screen mock-ups, saving 25 per cent of the time of the project according to Tom Jessiman. Moreover, 1UP.com's use of the wiki brought group e-mail down from a volume of 100 per day before using wikis to less than one a week.

Michelin China

Michelin is a vertically integrated global corporation which sells about 36,000 products, including tyres, wheels and inner tubes used on vehicles. Michelin China started using the open-source Twiki software in 2001 as they initiated a joint venture. They needed a tool for sharing project information within the project team and with people outside that team. While other tools were in use elsewhere in the company to share project information, they were difficult to use and put a significant content administration burden on project leaders.

The China information technology (IT) team started using a wiki as a knowledge management tool. Jean-Noel Simonnet writes, 'Our purpose was to share ALL the information, procedures, setup documents, so that we were less dependent on a particular staff member's knowledge, so that nobody in the team has any document left in a personal directory. Additionally and as our team is distributed across China, it gave us the ability to access content from any place.'[6]

Other departments looking for a tool to share data with their internal customers were also directed to the wiki. An IT user support space was consistently the most active wiki. Initially, a large number of pages were created by a few contributors, who were also the chief consumers of the information on the wikis. As time went on, the ratio of viewers to contributors grew. By 2004 the community of wiki users had grown to about 900 users and the wikis held a total of 1,600 pages.

Dresdner Kleinwort Wasserstein

Dresdner Kleinwort Wasserstein (DrKW) is an investment bank that provides capital markets and advisory services to corporate, institutional and government clients. Headquartered in London and Frankfurt with offices in a dozen other countries, it employs about 6,000 people.

DrKW installed their first wiki – an open source wiki – in 1997. Because of the large number of employees, their geographic distribution and the multiplicity of cultures, it had become essential to provide a variety of collaborative tools, from blogs and wikis to instant messenger, chat and audio/video conferencing. Rather than force people to use just one communications medium, the aim was to allow people to swap between modes, depending on which was most appropriate at the time.

Having become familiar with the opportunities afforded by a wiki, the IT department at DrKW decided to expand their support of wiki usage by installing a Socialtext system internally and creating a 'mother wiki', accessible to every employee and known as DrKWikipedia. Several other wikis were created and almost all of them grew over time and became frequently accessed and edited. The information strategy team was the first group to use Socialtext, followed by IT security; usage then rolled out to non-IT sections of the business.

The user-centred design (UCD) team, which works on the applications that DrKW develops, adopted the wiki as a communications tool, a collective discussion tool, as a repository for documents and information and as a project management tool. UCD members are also using the wiki to help inform a wider DrKW constituency of their activities, to explain what 'user-centred design' is and why it is important, as well as to share presentations, documents and reports.

A major user of wikis in DrKW is the Equity Delta1 equity financing team, whose members suffered from e-mail overload and moved most of their group discussions to topic-based wiki pages.[7] They also use the wiki to publish and share white papers and bulletins, for coordinating sales and marketing activities, and discussing and organising critical team tasks. The teams are still learning how best to use the wiki, and most still see it as an equivalent to shared folders and files rather than as a more versatile collaborative tool. There has also been resistance to the openness of the wiki. The Delta1 workspace is separate from the DrKWikipedia and might not have been adopted as rapidly without the privacy afforded by limited membership.

DrKW recently rolled wiki capacity out to over 4,000 users, but it is allowing uptake to develop gradually, providing informal training to encourage rather than enforce usage. Indeed, emergent use is accepted as a valuable part of the spread of wiki culture – one team's first use of the wiki was to organise their coffee rota, which they had previously done by e-mail. Reducing e-mail use even in such a seemingly trivial manner has a positive knock-on effect on users' productivity and ability to manage their workload by reducing the volume of non-essential messages. It also provides an innocuous 'practice run' that can facilitate the adoption of similar strategies in situations closer to core aspects of work. Over time, DrKW intends to use technologies, such as blogs, wikis and search to mould their entire approach to customer service and project planning. A detailed case study of the use of wikis at DrKW can be found on the Socialtext website.[8]

Prominent uses of wikis in business

Knowledge bases

Hidden within the wiki is a drive towards creating an internal glossary that will transform life, so if someone doesn't understand something they can look it up and find it defined not by a dictionary but by someone else doing a similar job. (JP Rangaswami, Global Head of Information Technology, Dresdner Kleinwort Wasserstein)[9]

The rapid development of Wikipedia over the past few years has been observed with a mixture of fascination and amazement. Wikipedia showcases online collaboration on an unprecedented scale – thousands of people are engaged in what Yochai Benkler calls commons-based peer production,[10] in which 'the creative energy of large numbers of people is coordinated into large, meaningful projects, largely without traditional hierarchical organisation or financial compensation'.[11] In many organisations, people have begun asking whether the model of work provided by Wikipedia might be emulated to build a shared internal knowledge base.

With work becoming more and more knowledge-intensive, there is a definite need for workers to be able to locate and reuse knowledge that already exists somewhere in their company. A lot of the really useful knowledge and know-how in the organisation is actually inside people's heads; when it is in a document, very often identifying the right document and its whereabouts requires tapping into someone's head. While people in smaller firms are sometimes able to get by through becoming acquainted with nearly everyone and being aware of what they know, in larger corporations people know only a fraction of their colleagues. Retrieving knowledge can become a problematic endeavour.

The idea of setting up a company-wide space where people can share their knowledge makes sense, and has been a key driver for the development of corporate intranets and knowledge management systems for more than a decade. Intranet deployments have, however, seen mixed success, in part owing to the difficulty of building and populating intranets and keeping them up to date. Employees do not always see adding or updating material in intranets as a priority, nor do they always take the time to send new or updated material to the webmaster or information architect in the organisations that have them. In this context, wikis make sense because they present a very low barrier to participation. A dramatic illustration of this is the case of Informative, Inc., where the move to a wiki reduced the time for new content to appear on the shared knowledge portal from 30 days to minutes.[12]

Another reason why corporate 'wikipedias' make sense is the fact that they are free-form. As such, they enable information that does not have a ready-made structure (e.g. 'Martha Smith knows where the non-disclosure agreements we signed in the last year are archived and organised') to be represented in a central, shared, searchable repository. Without a wiki, information such as this is often only transmitted in an ad hoc way, from person to person, through e-mail or face-to-face encounters. By searching a corporate wiki, someone who doesn't know about Martha and has no clue regarding her and the non-disclosure agreements, might be able to get a needed answer in minutes, without having to ask around and interrupt anybody in their work. This kind of information might be retrievable through the corporate intranet if a traditional corporate knowledge management system is being used diligently; however it might also only be the case that it falls through the cracks and is only present in the informal 'work traces' that exist in a wiki by virtue of its daily use in performing work. The fact that it supports the representation of informal knowledge also means that a corporate 'wikipedia' could be useful in helping newcomers to a company get up to speed without requiring as much one-on-one guidance from co-workers.

Another significant benefit of using a wiki for a knowledge base is that updating is so immediate that correcting mistakes or replacing outdated information is more within reach of everyone. This helps suppress the common scenario in intranets where a worker realises that a piece of information is stale and proceeds to find out the right information for their needs, but does not bother going through an involved process – possibly involving other people and delays – just to update the resource for future uses. The ease of updating a wiki can result in a resource that feels maintained and maintainable because many hands actually maintain it day-to-day.

Figure 5.1 gives a glimpse of how a sales team might use a wiki to keep up-to-date knowledge that is relevant to its operations. General information that is frequently needed by

Figure 5.1 The front page of a group wiki for a fictional sales team

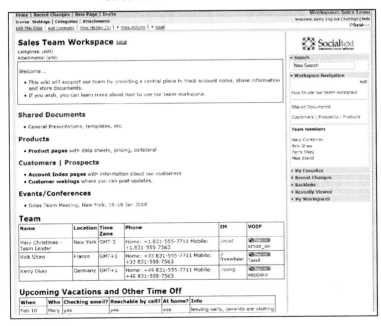

team members, such as contact information and items of current relevance, such as upcoming events and vacations, are best put directly on the front page. Separate pages may list shared documents, products, customers and prospects; each of these may in turn be documented on its own page.

The process that is used for sharing knowledge influences the content that is shared. As compared with a more traditional knowledge base predicated on a more involved process of drafting, revising, approving and only finally publishing information for common use, the extreme simplicity of the wiki process opens up contributions that may be less polished, but more genuine and authoritative. Says Marty Focazio, strategic services coordinator at Informative, 'When information is published, we know it's not from the hierarchy, it's from the person who knows what's going on'.[13]

In any knowledge sharing system, motivating participants to actually contribute is critical – the best-designed system is useless if it remains empty. Earning the trust and attention of colleagues through quality contributions is a powerful source of motivation. Wikis help raise the profile of skilled contributors in the company by giving team members the means to become the acknowledged expert in their area by sharing the results of their work. Those who happen to already be the acknowledged expert also welcome the wiki, as colleagues tend to solicit them heavily, thus the wiki makes it easy for them to publish answers to frequently asked questions. With a wiki, in the words of one Informative employee, 'I only have to answer a question once'.[14] At Stata Labs, building a wiki knowledge base collecting answers to recurring support requests resulted in a five-fold decrease in the number of required daily problem-solving conversations for front-line support workers.[15]

News monitoring and internal information dissemination

> The current options are too ..., er, blunt. You can always call someone in person and e-mail works for the entire group, but all the cases in between ... You know, when you need to reach a subset but you don't know exactly who ... That is difficult. (IT consultancy employee)[16]

The accelerating pace of change is an unmistakable trend in business. This demands increased awareness of relevant new developments on the part of workers. For a business, the needed awareness may be external: competitive intelligence and awareness of evolving markets and new technology, etc. are constant requirements in many sectors. Internal awareness – of strategies, plans, new opportunities – matters as well. On both counts, wikis can be helpful.

Wikis function effectively as central places to gather and efficiently share new knowledge coming in from outside the enterprise. Edward Williams, who heads the fraud and security department at a consumer bank, set up a number of wikis to help employees stay up to date and share information relating to security threats.[17] One of them focuses on threats targeting online banking customers, a fast-moving area requiring constant vigilance, with new scams appearing daily. Support workers use it as they work with customers for collaboratively building pictures of new threats and gathering related news. Another wiki was set up to keep the whole company up to date on issues of spam, social engineering and spyware.

Wiki participants can monitor new developments by regularly visiting the 'recent changes' list. Up to a certain level of activity, the company-wide recent changes list is able to keep people up to date with what is happening. However, given that not everyone in a company has the same information needs, as activity increases on a corporate wiki it will make sense for different people to pay attention to different information streams. Two of the most common ways to effect this are to create separate wikis and to use categories or weblogs (as indexes) to cluster pages together within a single wiki. Creating separate wikis has the advantage that it creates an implicit context or theme for pages. New pages created in a given wiki can be expected to relate to the overall theme of the wiki, so people may decide which wikis to monitor based on those themes.

On the other hand, keeping everything in a single wiki and using categories or weblogs has the advantage of keeping all information together in a central place, thereby avoiding the creation of islands of information and eliminating the question 'In which wiki is the information I need?' Centralising information can also lead to serendipitous interactions and to increasingly shared understanding of information. This option does, however, require more management, as categories must be added to pages or blogs need to be written (or both).

How does one know who is watching what? One enabling practice here is called the internal dashboard. It consists, quite simply, of a page where a person or a business unit lists and links to the wikis, categories and weblogs (if applicable) that they are watching regularly. For contributors, being aware of where other wiki participants' attention is directed can be very valuable. Dashboards increase the sense that someone is at the other end and encourage the funnelling of contributions into channels, which fosters interactions.

Used in conjunction with wikis, RSS readers can further accelerate the development of potent information flows all around an organisation. Users elect to subscribe to a number of web feeds, some of which may originate from general news sites out on the Web, while others may be internal feeds of recent changes from wikis or from specific pages, categories or weblogs within them. Once subscribed, users are automatically notified of any new content without having to repeatedly visit each source.

Project and group collaboration

> The project unfolded so much more smoothly because of the centralised, structured documentation available to all stakeholders via the wiki. Deadlines and roadblocks were clearly visible to all which helped us to avoid unnecessary delays. At the end of the project, we were left with a comprehensive record of its development; this enables us to review the overall success of our implementation and recognise any elements where we could have improved our service. (Janet Fisher, Ingenta Client Manager for McGraw-Hill)[18]

Another area where wikis prove helpful is in organising and documenting work at the team or project scale. There is especially significant potential when a group has a need for shared awareness, but is distributed or has members working at different times, so that bringing them together in real time in all-hands meetings proves difficult. A key benefit of using a wiki, once the tool is sufficiently woven into practices, is the ability for anyone to update information and be able to assume awareness on the part of others without calling a meeting or sending a message to everyone.

In the user-centred design team at Dresdner Kleinwort Wasserstein, the wiki has enabled the team to sidestep the problems associated with the previous practice of creating a traditional website for each project and has raised awareness across the team of what each person is doing, the status of each project and what actions need to be taken.

A number of artefacts are commonly built and updated in a wiki space by the members of a team to support its activities:

- *Descriptive pages.* A team summary table, typically found on the team wiki's homepage, lists members and key contact information:

  - *People pages* describe each person, with their picture, contact information, roles, usual schedule and links to projects they are involved in.

  - *Project summary pages* outline context, goals and requirements, players, key milestones and plans; they may also feature schedules and assignments of responsibility. Meeting notes, relevant research, contracts and other material that relates to the project may be linked from there.

- *Project weblogs.* Some wiki systems have built-in blogging systems. A project weblog is a way to keep updates together so that they are easy to follow and reference. Blog posts can link to web resources and project documents within the workspace, situating conversations in the project context, unlike e-mail threads where the context is difficult to discover. The weblog helps team members communicate and gives managers a means of being aware of ongoing work, without adding an extra step to the process.

- *Event calendar.* A table listing upcoming events along with their dates. When somebody learns of a new event or a significant date is determined, one simply adds a row to the calendar. Event names may link to pages with further detail.

- *Records and support materials for meetings.* Prior to a meeting or phone conference, an agenda is drafted on a wiki page and people are invited to add to it. During the meeting, people can jot down meeting notes in real time and make them available instantly to others.

- *Collaboratively-written documents.* The wiki becomes the obvious place to draft and review all kinds of texts: documentation, specifications, marketing copy, etc. The need for e-mail back-and-forth between participants is considerably reduced, and because of the transparency of the wiki, other team members who otherwise wouldn't have been involved may look on and help improve the result without having to cope with an additional e-mail burden from the collaboration process.

Conclusion

This chapter has given an overview of uses of wikis in business environments. Wikis differ from most other enterprise software in that they offer simplicity, an open, unconstrained publishing model that supports informal communication and drives attention toward content and links. Inside organisations, they are evolving from an application that was mostly used by software developers, to a general-purpose collaborative tool that is being applied in a wide array of work contexts, in some cases supporting mission-critical information, without losing the simplicity that made them popular. We presented specific uses of wiki technology at Ziff Davis Media, Michelin China and Dresdner Kleinwort Wasserstein. Finally, we described how wikis are helping with news monitoring and information dissemination, in cooperatively creating and shaping knowledge bases and in project and group collaboration.

Wiki usage is still growing and diversifying, and there is no doubt that a variety of suitable new applications will be identified as more people gain awareness of the technology and embrace wikis to help get things done together.

Notes

1. Socialtext, 'Stata Labs: Managing at a Distance, for Less'; available at: *http://www.socialtext.com/customers/ customerstata/* (accessed: 23 December 2005).

2. Venners, B. (2003) 'Exploring with wiki: a conversation with Ward Cunningham', *Artima Developer*; available at: *http://www.artima.com/intv/wiki.html* (accessed: 11 February 2006).

3. Gilbane Report (2005) 'Survey on enterprise, blog and wiki use', *Gilbane Report*; available at: *http://gilbane.com/ surveys.html* (accessed: 11 February 2005).

4. Thoeny, P. and Woods, D. (2005) 'Book on wikis in the workplace'; available at: *http://twiki.org/cgi-bin/view/Codev/ WikisInTheWorkplaceBook* (page dated 20:52, 7 December 2005; accessed: 11 February 2006).

5. Socialtext, 'Ziff Davis Media accelerates project cycles and reduces group e-mails from 100 per day to zero'; available at: *http://www.socialtext.com/customers/customerziff* (accessed: 23 December 2005).

6. Simonnet, J.-N. (2004) 'Twiki success story of Michelin China'; available at: *http://twiki.org/cgi-bin/view/Main/ TWikiSuccessStoryOfMichelinChina* (page dated 17:42, 2 December 2004; accessed: 11 February 2006).

7. Conlin, M. (2005) 'E-mail is so five minutes ago', *Business Week Online*, 28 November; available at: *http://www .businessweek.com/magazine/content/05_48/b3961120.htm* (accessed: 23 December 2005).

8. Socialtext, 'Dresdner Kleinwort Wasserstein case study'; available at: *http://www.socialtext.com/customers/ customerdrkw/* (accessed: 23 December 2005).

9. Ibid.
10. Benkler, Y. (2002) 'Coase's penguin, or, Linux and the nature of the firm', *Yale Law Journal* 112(3): 369–446. Unpaginated version at; available at: *http://www.benkler.org/CoasesPenguin.html* (accessed: 11 February 2006).
11. Wikipedia (2005) 'Commons-based peer production'; available at: *http://en.wikipedia.org/wiki/Peer_production* (page dated 09:57, 14 December 2005; accessed: 31 January 2006).
12. Socialtext, 'An informative intranet and people's portal'; available at: *http://www.socialtext.com/customers/customerinformative* (accessed: 23 December 2005).
13. Ibid.
14. Ibid.
15. Socialtext, 'Stata Labs: managing at a distance, for less'; available at: *http://www.socialtext.com/customers/customerstata* (accessed: 23 December 2005).
16. Stenmark, D. (2005) 'Knowledge sharing on a corporate intranet: effects of re-instating web authoring capability', *Proceedings of ECIS 2005, Regensburg, Germany, 26–28 May 2005*; available at: *http://www.informatik.gu.se/~dixi/publ/ecis_27.pdf* (accessed: 14 January 2006).
17. Delio, M. (2005) 'Enterprise collaboration with blogs and wikis', *Infoworld*, 25 March; available at: *http://www.infoworld.com/article/05/03/25/13FEblogwiki_1.html* (accessed: 11 February 2006).
18. Ingenta (2005) 'Wiki Wiki What?' *Eye to Eye* 12 (March); available at: *http://eyetoeye.ingenta.com/publisher/issue12/insight-wiki.htm* (accessed: 23 December 2005).

6

Wikis in education
Pru Mitchell

This chapter focuses on the ways wikis can be used in education and considers the two major functions of wikis introduced in earlier chapters: wikis as information sources and wikis as social information spaces. While different in purpose and application, both these functions of wiki technology can be applied in schools, technical education and higher education institutions. This chapter presents examples of wikis developed for students, educators, researchers and education administrators. The nature of wiki technology can create special issues for the education sector and strategies for addressing these challenges are discussed.

Overview

From the early history of online applications in education there has been a perceived hierarchy, or continuum, of online activity, which leads learners from online discovery (browsing), through searching, to online communication and collaboration and finally to publishing online.[1] While wikis are very much part of the collaborative Web, there remains a logic to taking a developmental approach to a new online technology. Before contributing to, or creating a wiki, educators and their students can develop an understanding of wikis by browsing and reading them, and by using them as an information tool.

Wikis as information tools in education

Wikis are causing a redefinition of what constitutes an authoritative or quality information source. Some argue that wikis are the tried and trusted system of peer review taken to a new level. Others point to a wiki covered in spam to justify their stance against the use of wikis as valid sources of information in education. For many, wikis have become yet another reason to stress the importance of teaching critical literacy and the need to develop information literacy for all students and staff. While Chapter 2 provides an overview of wiki-based information tools, the next few pages discuss particular issues and examples of wikis as reference sources for students and educators.

Wikipedia

http://www.wikipedia.org

The best-known wiki, the open-source encyclopaedia, Wikipedia, is the first experience of a wiki for many people. Although it was introduced in Chapter 2, it is worth discussing specific issues associated with the use of Wikipedia in education.

Wikipedia rates highly in search engines for many search terms and to the wiki newbie it looks little different from a traditional informational website. A number of the people who use Wikipedia as an information source do not even realise that it is a wiki, or how it differs from a traditional online encyclopaedia or information source.

The following questions arise: can you trust Wikipedia and can Wikipedia be accepted as a legitimate source in an academic work? According to Wikipedia, it has been cited in published academic writing since 2002[2] and it is common to find links to Wikipedia on university websites, as well as in government policy documents. Wikipedia has a schools' FAQ[3] which attempts to address the questions asked by educators and students regarding use of Wikipedia as an information tool. Is it accurate and reliable, what keeps someone from contributing false or misleading information and is it a safe environment for young people, are some of the major frequently asked questions (FAQs) covered. Prensky[4] suggests educators teach about, rather than ban Wikipedia 'just because it might not be as correct or accurate as a traditional encyclopaedia written by paid experts. If that's our criterion for what kids can read and cite, we'd better re-think kids' access to the Bible!' Let's give the final word to a school that has grappled with the Wikipedia dilemma:

> Students like it because the language is accessible and there is often a considerable amount of information on more obscure topics. In the end, our advice to students was to treat it as an unverified source – i.e. check the facts against reputable reference sources. (Portside Christian School Library)[5]

Wikinews

http://www.wikinews.org

Wikinews, a collection of news reports written collaboratively by members of the public, can, like

Wikipedia, be a useful source of information for educators and students. It is discussed in more detail in Chapter 2.

Wikibooks

http://en.wikibooks.org/wiki

Wikibooks were also introduced in Chapter 2. They are free, open-content textbooks and manuals compiled by 'Wikibookians', who are not necessarily educators. Users can add a request for a textbook they would like to see and the wish lists include business and computing topics as well as learning a foreign language or a sport. Wikibooks readers are informed that they 'will never have to wait months or years for another edition to come out that incorporates the latest changes in the field. The very minute a discovery or advancement is made the text can be updated to reflect that change'.[6]

Wikis as tools for collaboration in the educational setting

While wikis can be interesting and useful personal management tools and sources of information, it is the collaborative, creative nature of the wiki that holds the real power for education. Wiki software enables educators to provide learning opportunities with increased interactivity, authenticity and social purpose. Background discussion of wikis as social software is provided in Chapter 1. Included here is a short discussion of pedagogy relevant to wikis, and examples of educators using wikis for a variety of purposes, such as to enhance student learning, for professional collaboration, for collaborative writing and research, and to manage information and projects across institutional and geographic boundaries.

Wikis and collaborative pedagogy

The potential impact of information and communications technology (ICT) on education has been a hot topic for some time, with ongoing debate as to whether it is realising its potential to change, or more importantly, improve learning, particularly in terms of its social and communications value. UNESCO documents, such as *Learning without Frontiers*,[7] point to learning technologies as having the capacity to support a genuine social constructivist approach, as well as promising improved global access to education. Guzdial explains a potential impact of wiki technology as changing the teacher–student relationship. 'Learning scientists refer to this phenomenon as "shifting the agency". In most classrooms, the teacher has the "agency", the control, the driving force – the teacher asks the questions, the students respond. But in the real world, each of us have our own agency'. [8]

Recent commentators have stressed the importance of networks and their contribution to learning. Surowiecki's book *The Wisdom of Crowds*[9] considers the concept of collective wisdom and why the judgments of the many are, in many cases, better than the judgments of individuals. Siemens explores a concept of 'connectivism', describing it as 'the integration of principles explored by chaos, network, and complexity and self-organisation theories. Learning is a process that occurs within nebulous environments of shifting core elements – not entirely under the control of the individual'.[10] The wiki is a technology that can facilitate the approaches to learning inherent in theories such as collective wisdom and connectivism.

As with any teaching tool or resource, a wiki being used in education must also reflect good practice in terms of instructional design, functionality and usability. Fountain warns educators: 'just bringing in a new tool does not change practice. Co-elaboration and cooperation will not simply occur because wikis are introduced to one's practice'. [11]

Wikis in the collaborative classroom

Students will not simply pass through a course like water through a sieve but instead leave their own imprint in the development of the course, their school or university and ideally the discipline. (Holmes et al.)[12]

This vision of learning promoted by Holmes and colleagues seems an ideal base from which to consider how a class or course-based wiki can promote collaboration and provide opportunities for student-centred, connected learning. We consider three issues – socialisation, group work and assessment – before providing examples of wikis in the classroom.

Particularly important to successful use of a wiki in a class are the first two stages of Salmon's five-stage model of online activity:[13] (1) access and motivation, and (2) online socialisation. Allowing sufficient time for students to develop a sense of community or network is a major success indicator in online activities and Augar, Raitman and Zhou suggest using a wiki as an icebreaker activity for online learning groups.[14] Wikis also have the potential to motivate students. In education, it can be difficult to provide a practical and authentic audience for student writing, but the ease of editing a wiki from anywhere can make it easier for people outside the class to be part of the experience. It is also feasible for students and teachers to develop material within their private class wiki and then contribute it to another wiki, particularly for topics where students have not found appropriate online and print resources already available to meet their needs.

Wikis are used in project-based learning and group assignments, either at the brainstorming and refining topic stage, throughout the assignment, or as a presentation tool at the end of the learning process. Use of the linking functionality within a wiki is particularly powerful in helping students make connections between their particular topic and what other students in the class are contributing. Some teachers mandate linking to, or contributing to, other class or team pages as part of the assignment, while others develop templates or prompts to provide scaffolding for new users.[15]

A wiki can provide authentic and rapid feedback to contributors, and having others edit one's work in ongoing collaborative writing is a powerful learning experience. A wiki can be used for students and teachers to develop checklists, assessment criteria or rubrics for an upcoming learning activity, or as a self-evaluation or peer assessment tool. The issue of 'counting' who contributed what content to a class wiki can be problematic when working in teams unless each student logs in separately. Teachers and students will need to discuss whether teamwork is to be assessed collectively or on an individual basis. Raman, Ryan and Olfman report on the challenge of assessing quality as opposed to quantity of content in a class wiki, finding in their research that 30 per cent of students in one class contributed approximately 75 per cent of the knowledge.[16]

Our Changing Times (the miniLegends wiki)

http://www.seedwiki.org/wiki/ourchangingtimes/ourchangingtimes.cfm

Al Upton at Glenelg School, South Australia, developed this wiki to explore '*Our Changing Times* ... what you like about being a kid in 2004 and what was it like for other generations in the last 100 years' with year 3 students. Upton now uses the Our Changing Times wiki for demonstration purposes in his role as a 'learning with the Internet' coach (see Figure 6.1).[17]

Figure 6.1   Sample page from Glenelg School Our Changing Times: miniLegends wiki

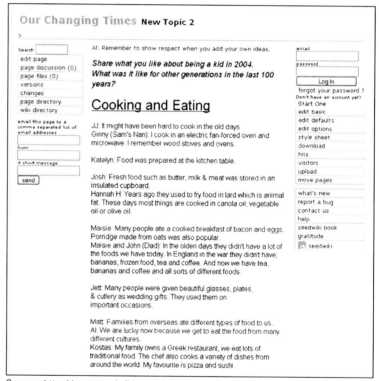

Source: *http://www.seedwiki.org/wiki/ourchangingtimes/new_topic_2.cfm? wpid=168724*

Matt Barton TikiWiki

http://www.mattbarton.net/tikiwiki/tiki-index.php

Matt Barton uses a wiki as the website for his teaching of English at St. Cloud State University in Minnesota. The site incorporates blogs, forums and wikis to which students contribute.

An Introduction to Digital Environments for Learning

http://www.malts.ed.ac.uk/idel/assignment/wiki

Lange and Paterson used a wiki in the teaching of their 2005 University of Edinburgh course entitled *An Introduction to Digital Learning Environments*.[18] There is a useful section, 'Using a Wiki for a Collaborative Essay' that discusses issues and benefits of this style of assignment and some examples of the use of wikis in teaching.

Wiki for IS Scholarship

http://isworld.student.cwru.edu/tiki/tiki-index.php

The Information Systems Department at the Weatherhead School of Management at Case Western Reserve University has developed a wiki where doctoral students summarise and discuss articles related to the field of information systems.

Visual Design Tutorial

http://nearlythere.com/cgi-bin/design/wiki.cgi?

A 'tutorial about web design for non-experts' is the description given to this part of the Nearly There wiki maintained by Heather James. It is a completed wiki, the development of which is discussed in James' article on using a wiki in her class.[19] The wiki is now locked as the site explains, 'the design class was complete and everyone lived happily ever after'. There is a useful WikisInEducation page that includes a list of links to other sites discussing the use of wikis in education.

Wikis and collaborative professional learning

This section considers use of wikis for professional collaboration and professional learning among educators, whether in a formal course or training scenario, or an informal learning community. Applications include the development and management of e-portfolios, facilitation of peer reviews and the development of communities of practice. We provide some examples of wikis in these categories.

E-portfolios

Reflection is a key component of learning. While weblogs are often the tool of choice for personal online learning journals, wikis work well as an e-portfolio tool, providing flexibility in layout and structure, and the ability to hold images and multimedia if required. Portfolio development can be undertaken by individual students and educators, or in class, staff or faculty teams; in addition, a wiki may be used for the process of developing the portfolio, to hold the finished product, or both. While the e-portfolio is a strategy for documenting learning and professional growth, an e-portfolio that incorporates a wiki enhances this by allowing peers, employers or students to comment on material documented in the portfolio.

UBC Teaching e-Portfolio

http://ubcteachingeportfolio.notlong.com

From the University of British Columbia, this wiki about e-portfolios includes examples of teaching e-portfolios, plus resources, tips and FAQs.

Peer review

The value of feedback and peer review is recognised by those who use wikis with students, and it is also worth exploring by educators in terms of their own professional development. The 'anyone can edit' nature of the peer review function available in a wiki raises debate in academic circles, with reference particularly to popular wiki sites, such as Wikipedia. This is less of an issue, however, for a wiki with a specific academic audience, or one whose use is limited to a particular education community. If an educator posts a draft of a lesson or course, an article or other professional document to a wiki, feedback or a formal review can be invited quickly and simply from the audience of that particular wiki. The reviewers themselves can be informed by how others are reviewing the work, and the potential for discussion and debate can lead to an improved review process.

Communities of practice

Moving beyond the personal learning emphasis of e-portfolios and peer-reviewed writing, Godwin-Jones suggests that wikis may be ideal for building communities of practice by creating a collective repository of expertise in a subject area. The repository is refined over time by the contributions and problem-solving of interested individuals.[20] If communities of practice can be nurtured in the online environment, Bulfin believes that social technology, such as wikis, could assist early career teachers and practitioner-researchers to talk and write about their professional learning, enabling them to look for professional conversations beyond the immediate context of their own school.[21]

Adult Literacy Education (ALE) Wiki

http://wiki.literacytent.org

With the inspiring motto: 'We're workers, not lurkers', this wiki created by David Rosen encourages adult literacy educators to 'learn about the field here and also contribute your knowledge from research, experience teaching adult learners, or your experience as an adult learner'. It provides over 20 discussion topics from accountability to young adult literacy and provides a 'WhosHere' directory of participants.

Connectivism

http://www.connectivism.ca/wiki

George Siemens provides a wiki for discussion of connectivism. It includes support material for presentations, including one titled 'Cool-Connections' that discusses the problems that a network-view of learning can solve – problems of relevance in a world defined by 'complexity, continual change, information abundance and distributed knowledge/learning/cognition'.[22]

WikEd

http://wik.ed.uiuc.edu

This wiki is provided as a service to the education community by the Curriculum, Technology & Education

Reform (CTER) programme at the University of Illinois. It invites educators to create and edit pages and includes articles and links on a wide range of educational psychology and educational technology topics, including topic pages contributed by students studying psychology of classroom learning and management and a book entitled *Blended Learning in K12* co-created by faculty and masters students.

Ti Wiki

http://wiki.tertiary.govt.nz/

Ti Wiki is a collaborative website for the New Zealand (NZ) Tertiary Education Sector. Its focus is information and information-related issues. Also hosted here is the NZ Schools (e)Learning Wiki.

Teacher Librarians Meeting Space

http://www.groups.edna.edu.au/course/view.php?id=5

The Teacher Librarians Meeting Space is a free online play space for teacher librarians interested in trialling collaborative tools. It is hosted by EdNA Groups, a collaborative workspace built on Moodle.[23] The TL wiki provides a platform for teacher librarians to share and develop reading lists, units of work and procedures documentation. Resources in the TL wiki in 2005 included the 'read alouds' booklist, toys unit of work, staff holiday reading booklist and a list of picture books about courage. Figure 6.2 illustrates the range of workspaces operating in the wiki.

Figure 6.2 A sample of the workspaces in the EdNA Teacher Librarians Meeting Space wiki

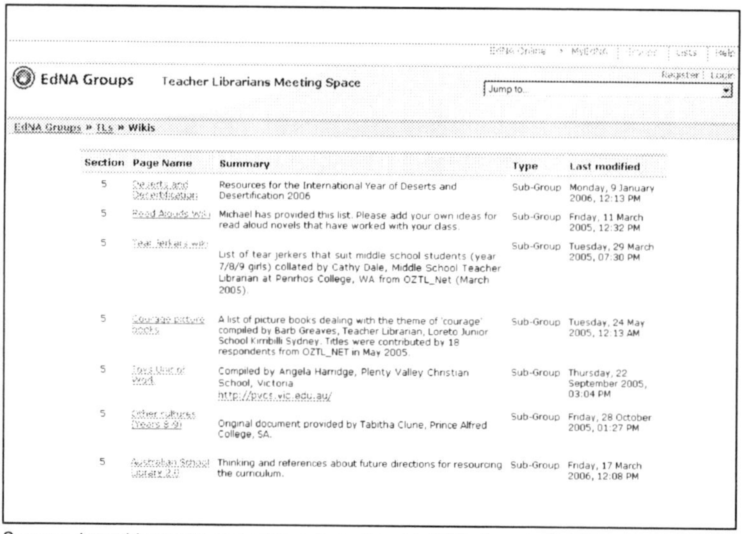

Section	Page Name	Summary	Type	Last modified
5	Deserts and Desertification	Resources for the International Year of Deserts and Desertification 2006	Sub-Group	Monday, 9 January 2006, 12:13 PM
5	Read Alouds Wiki	Michael has provided this list. Please add your own ideas for read aloud novels that have worked with your class.	Sub-Group	Friday, 11 March 2005, 12:32 PM
5	Tear Jerkers wiki	List of tear jerkers that suit middle school students (year 7/8/9 girls) collated by Cathy Dale, Middle School Teacher Librarian at Penrhos College, WA from OZTL_Net (March 2005).	Sub-Group	Tuesday, 29 March 2005, 07:30 PM
5	Courage picture books	A list of picture books dealing with the theme of 'courage' compiled by Barb Greaves, Teacher Librarian, Loreto Junior School Kirribilli Sydney. Titles were contributed by 18 respondents from OZTL_NET in May 2005.	Sub-Group	Tuesday, 24 May 2005, 12:13 AM
5	Toys Unit of Work	Compiled by Angela Harridge, Plenty Valley Christian School, Victoria http://pvcs.vic.edu.au/	Sub-Group	Thursday, 22 September 2005, 03:04 PM
5	Other cultures (Years 8-9)	Original document provided by Tabitha Clune, Prince Alfred College, SA.	Sub-Group	Friday, 28 October 2005, 01:27 PM
5	Australian School Library 2.0	Thinking and references about future directions for resourcing the curriculum.	Sub-Group	Friday, 17 March 2006, 12:08 PM

Source: *http://www.groups.edna.edu.au/mod/wiki/index.php?id=5*

Wikis and collaborative content development

Collaborative writing is the basic function of the wiki from which all other applications can be seen to derive. The nature of that writing may be a diverse range of information products or knowledge artefacts. Educators and learners can collaboratively construct a range of factual and creative material, from group writing assignments, class presentations, policy and procedures documentation, test questions, course and curriculum content, to newsletters, magazines or a school history.

Writing process

As a public and very open text-based medium with the ability to track editing history, the contribution of multiple authors and the areas of disagreement and consensus, Allison regards the wiki as an ideal resource for studying and teaching about the writing process.[24] The wide variety of genres represented in the wiki format gives a rich source of material for the study of text types, such as procedures, reviews, explanation, parody, social comment and news stories. Concepts, such as voice and point of view, are easily illustrated in wikis. Students of journalism can follow a news story and study editing history on a wiki news service, and students have many examples on which to model their own written responses and reviews. Unlike traditional HTML or presentation software, wikis emphasise content rather than the formatting and flashy presentation that can sidetrack younger students when they are creating and publishing online.

Curriculum development

Distance education academics and instructional designers have been working collaboratively to write and prepare course materials for many years. The content and interpersonal aspects of this process are equally relevant to the use of a wiki in the co-creation of courses. However, a collaborative online writing tool, such as a wiki, can bring significant improvement in practicality and timeliness. The elimination of multiple versions of draft materials sitting on different personal computers and moving around via e-mail is a huge benefit of writing via a wiki.

Use of wikis for collaborative content development applies beyond traditional text-oriented content, with uptake by designers using wikis for storyboarding multimedia presentations and computer science students developing collaborative programming code.

Lesson Plan Sandbox

http://avc.comm.nsdlib.org/Education/lesson_plan_sandbox .shtml

The Lesson Plan Sandbox is part of the National Science Digital Library (see Chapter 4). It is an environment for collaborative development of lesson plans in the areas of earth science, technology, physical sciences, space sciences, process skills, applied mathematics and meteorology using atmospheric radiation measurement data. The introduction to a sample lesson plan, developed by the Argonne National Laboratory, appears in Figure 6.3.

Wikis and collaborative research

While original research is specifically excluded in the content policies of Wikipedia where verifiability is prized, an increasing number of wikis do provide a forum for those

Figure 6.3 Introduction to 'Comparing temperature, pressure and humidity' lesson plan in the NSDL Lesson Plan Sandbox

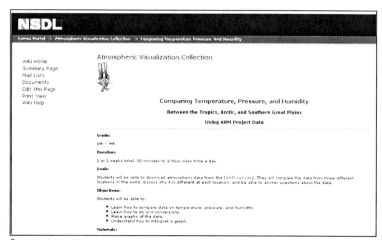

Source: *http://avc.comm.nsdlib.org/Education/lesson_plan_sandbox.shtml*

involved in research. Wikis are used for building a literature review, storing data, inviting qualitative responses from subjects and publishing. They also enable members to share work with other researchers and increase awareness of the global community in a particular specialisation. According to Fountain, 'the peer review process so highly valued in academia has been seriously challenged by wiki's open authorisation' as wikis are beginning to be seen as at least a supplement to, if not replacement for, peer review journals, offering a broader and more timely discussion than is possible in print and conference research forums.[25] However, within a competitive research funding landscape, it can be difficult for institutions to conduct their research and development activity within such a collaborative philosophy. Thus, researchers may be restricted to a public wiki that shares links to review literature, references and public output, while their data and unpublished material remain on private institutional servers.

OpenWetWare

http://openwetware.org

OpenWetWare is the wiki of a group of American researchers, labs and groups working in biology and biological engineering. They share information about each other's activities, courses and other know-how. The wiki provides access to shared resources in areas ranging from computing to cloning vectors.

Veronica Research Group Wiki

Veronica is an international group of researchers conducting a longitudinal case study of change in a development aid consulting firm as it attempts to use the Internet to support communication and culture among its widely distributed staff. Veronica's members are in Italy, Denmark and Australia, and individual members are often travelling. The group uses a number of collaborative tools, including a wiki, to support their research. A private wiki, hosted at JotSpot,[26] is used primarily to keep track of events that occur during the study period and that may influence the results of the research. As members of Veronica hear about new appointments, changes in staff location, strategy planning activities, new technologies, visits and courses, they add it to the history page of the wiki. In due course, the Veronica project will be described in a book. A wiki is being used to develop the outline of the book and each chapter – much as the authors of this book used a wiki to develop outlines and share resources during the initial stages of writing. A screen shot of the book development page appears in Figure 6.4.

Figure 6.4 Veronica Research Group book development wiki page

Wikis for collaborative knowledge repositories

The previously discussed models of wiki use in education are about learning, knowledge creation and knowledge development within a community. Wiki technology is also appropriate for storing knowledge once created. The 'edit anywhere' nature of a wiki makes it very convenient for storing links to resource material, compiling an online bibliography or collating a group reading list. Wikis are often used to develop and store FAQs, and this is an activity that students can take ownership of in a class situation. Policy and procedures documentation is also easily published and readily edited by appropriate staff. The ability to include a wiki-based discussion about such documents prompts ongoing review and editing. Within an educational environment or organisation that does not have access to an alternative content management system, a wiki can provide a timely, convenient way for posting breaking news, daily notices or events notifications by allowing members of the community to post readily from any web-enabled computer.

Project management

Within a community there are applications for wikis in administration and project management activity. In an increasingly globalised education environment, collaborative conference planning using a wiki is becoming popular, particularly within the higher education sector, as it enables planning and programme committees to be truly international and include representation from the key thinkers in a particular field. The whole process from programme planning, the call for papers, administrative assistance and publishing of conference proceedings can be managed through a conference wiki. Document storage and knowledge archiving is another area where wikis are well used.

DCMI Education Working Group Wiki

http://dublincore.org/educationwiki

An example of a wiki that enables collaboration across institutional and geographic boundaries, the Dublin Core Education Working Group Wiki is the primary mechanism for reporting on the ongoing activities of this metadata working group. Current activities on the DC-Ed Wiki include work plans, FAQs, agendas, notes, documentation and links to key references for taskforces.

HigherEd BlogCon

http://higheredblogcon.editme.com/

HigherEd BlogCon is a web-based conference that aims to bring together leaders in the educational use of the social Web. The conference website demonstrates the use of a wiki for conference planning and management by a geographically diverse committee.

Issues in implementing educational wikis

The information on how to create a wiki in Chapter 7 and discussion of wiki management in Chapter 8 covers major issues in implementing wikis. This section addresses aspects that may be of particular importance, or specific to, the education context.

Why wiki?

The preceding discussion has identified many applications of wikis in education and examples of educators who have found value in using wikis. However, in considering whether the implementation of an emerging technology, such as wikis is appropriate in a particular education context, educators need to map benefits and issues against relevant local strategic plans as well as functional requirements. *Emerging technologies*[27] suggests a decision-making matrix be used to guide this process covering the following eight issues:

- teaching and learning outcomes;
- teacher acceptance;
- student acceptance and parental support;
- leadership in use and take-up;
- relevant, available and cost effective content;
- sustainability, resourcing, risk, extensibility;
- interoperability and integration;
- applicability.

Which wiki?

Paths and questions to guide selection of wiki software are discussed in Chapter 7. The educational environment offers some particular opportunities for adoption of wikis. Moodle[28] is an open source course management system being used increasingly in education which contains a wiki as a major module. Vendors, such as Microsoft also expect to include wikis as part of their core collaborative environment, centred on applications, such as SharePoint.[29] Schwartz and colleagues at Athabasca University[30] present a wiki selection criteria document to help those selecting a wiki for educational use. Of the long list of features available in some wikis, those using wikis with students need to carefully consider password protection and spam handling functionality to maximise the potential for a positive and productive learning experience. Extensions are also being developed to facilitate the class use of wikis, such as Wang's[31] timer to address the issue of simultaneous editing within a class wiki. With the timer, if a user tries to access the edit page while another user is currently editing it, then a timer is set for the current page editor.

How to wiki?

Safety

The unique and somewhat anarchic nature of wikis makes them interesting and powerful tools for educators involved in developing student awareness of information literacy, critical literacy and information ethics. However, as with blogging, there is debate about whether educational wiki installations, particularly those in schools, should be restricted to internal use to minimise access to undesirable content and behaviour. Each community will need to balance the educational benefits and duty of care risks of providing an 'authentic' open wiki experience versus restricted, safe wiki use.

Wikiquette

While educators introducing a wiki as a writing tool may like to emphasise the freedom of expression provided by the wiki, at some point the need for a commonly accepted style guide and rules of engagement will become apparent, as for any written project. This style guide can itself be developed as a wiki, enabling all contributors to raise questions, make suggestions and draft guidelines, although the time limitations placed upon students in a course may lead educators to provide an initial style guide up front. Many wikis have their own style guides or writing rules, which provide students with a model of 'real world' assessment criteria. Existing content or netiquette (Internet communication etiquette) guidelines can be adapted to cover educational wikis, perhaps with a reminder that all members of the wiki community share responsibility for moderating content. If a wiki is to have a rating or reward system, the criteria for this will also need to be agreed upon.

Information ethics

Information ethics issues apply to wikis as for all academic writing, although the community in which the wiki is used has more influence on the application of these ethics than is possible in other forms of publishing. Information literacy skills need explicit attention so that consumers of information from wikis understand that the onus is on the user to verify and validate facts, statistics and histories from other sources. Creators and contributors should appreciate the benefit of accurate acknowledgment of their sources, and students will also benefit from discussion of a set of criteria for evaluating wiki content.

Referencing

As students, educators and researchers need to include references from wikis in their writing, the issue of how to cite these in academic work needs to be addressed. Consistency with the institution's recommended citation style is required, whether that be Harvard, APA or local guidelines. As with any new publication medium, it takes some time for a standard format of citation to develop, refine and be accepted. Wiki pages will be cited in similar ways to web pages, encyclopaedia articles or journal articles. The major issues for wiki citation centre on *dates* and *authorship*. Suggestions for dealing with these issues are provided in Chapter 2.

Intellectual property

In terms of intellectual property, wikis represent a major shift in the concept of personal ownership of ideas. Although it may be possible to identify an individual's ideas or content in a wiki, it is the community's acceptance and ownership that has most validity in the wiki environment. The reality of wikis is that contributions can easily be copied directly from other sources, including commercial, copyright protected publications and pasted into a wiki without acknowledgment. While this is no different from plagiarism in other educational and publication formats, the sheer scale of contribution to a major wiki site makes monitoring particularly difficult for the wiki community. Much material in public wikis is published under licences that permit reuse with appropriate acknowledgment. Educators will also have to consider the reality of students using a wiki community to write or edit work that is then handed in for assessment. What constitutes 'fair use' of wiki content will need to be checked with the legal jurisdiction of the particular educational institution. Freedom of expression questions may also vary between jurisdictions and those publishing online are urged to familiarise themselves with what constitutes legal and acceptable practice.

Who wikis?

Maximising the social and collaborative potential of wikis is the major challenge for educators implementing wikis. While the technology aims to be simple, the reality of building online communities and managing social interactions can be complex, requiring an understanding of the social software phenomena and the importance of social norms in wiki communities. A study of how and why wikis do or do not work is tied up in personality, group dynamics, knowledge construction, trust and socialisation. Why do some people volunteer to contribute to or manage open source projects while others look for opportunities to profit personally from public domain material? What motivates online vandals and spammers?

Preece[32] describes four basic online community roles that apply to the wiki environment. While moderators have an overall or whole group function, perhaps as the teacher or sponsor of a wiki, role models, often early members of the community or leaders, help new members by explaining and commenting, and providing feedback on content. Mentors might be used to greet new members and offer social and cultural support rather than content, while the role of citizen regulation is shared in a wiki where everyone takes responsibility for deletion of vandalism and possibly for the expulsion of members. While roles in wiki use reflect other online community tools, some specific language has also arisen. WikiMaster is a common term for a wiki administrator, although in the school setting, WikiMonitor may be pertinent, while cricket fans may prefer WikiKeeper.[33]

Notes

1. Mitchell, P. (1996) 'Online technology in the curriculum: a reality', in *Beyond the Horizon, Proceedings of the 14th Biennial Conference of the Australian School Library Association*, West Perth, Western Australia; pp: 185–98.

2. Wikipedia (2006) 'Wikipedia: Wikipedia as an academic source'; available at: *http://en.wikipedia.org/wiki/Wikipedia: Wikipedia_as_an_academic_source* (page dated: 16:03, 16 February 2006; accessed: 19 February 2006).

3. Wikipedia (2006) 'Wikipedia: Schools' FAQ'; available at: *http://en.wikipedia.org/wiki/Wikipedia:Schools_FAQ* (page dated: 01:17, 18 February 2006; accessed: 19 February 2006).

4. Prensky, M. (2005) 'Search vs. research or, the fear of the Wikipedia overcome by new understanding for a digital era'; available at: *http://www.marcprensky.com/writing/Prensky-Search_vs_Research-01.pdf* (accessed: 15 January 2006).

5. Portside Christian School Library (2005) 'Beware the wiki', *OZTL_NET* 5; available at: *http://listserv.csu.edu.au/ mailman/private/oztl_net/2005-December/023307.html* (accessed: 15 December 2005.

6. Wikibooks (2006) 'Wikibooks: why use open textbooks'; available at: *http://en.wikibooks.org/wiki/Why_use_open_ textbooks%3F* (page dated: 11:20, 17 February 2006; accessed: 18 February 2006).

7. Learning Without Frontiers (1999) 'Learning without frontiers: constructing open learning communities for lifelong learning'. UNESCO; available at: *http://www.unesco.org/ education/lwf/* (accessed: 15 January 2006).

8. Guzdial, M. (2005) as quoted in D. Mattison (2005) 'Swiki words', *Searcher* 11(4): 43; available at: *http://www .infotoday.com/searcher/apr03/mattison.shtml* (accessed: 15 January 2006).

9. Surowiecki, J. (2004) *The Wisdom of Crowds*. New York: Doubleday.

10. Siemens, G. 'Cool-connections'; available at: *http://www. connectivism.ca/wiki/CoolConnections* (undated page; accessed: 18 February 2006).

11. Fountain, R. (2005) 'Wiki pedagogy', *Dossiers technopédagogiques*; available at: *http://www.profetic.org: 16080/dossiers/rubrique.php3?id_rubrique=110* (accessed: 15 January 2006).

12. Holmes, B., Tangney, B., FitzGibbon, A., Savage, T. and Mehan, S. (2001) 'Communal constructivism: Students

constructing learning for as well as with others', *12th International Conference of the Society for Information Technology and Teacher Education (SITE)*; available at: *https://www.cs.tcd.ie/publications/tech-reports/reports.01/ TCD-CS-2001-04.pdf* (accessed: 15 January 2006).

13. Salmon, G. (2004) 'All things in moderation'; available at: *http://www.atimod.com/e-tivities/5stage.shtml* (accessed: 15 January 2006).

14. Augar, N., Raitman, R. and Zhou, W. (2004) 'Teaching and learning online with wikis', in *Beyond the Comfort Zone: Proceedings of the 21st Annual Conference of the Australasian Society for Computers in Learning in Tertiary Education (ASCILITE)*; pp: 95–104; available at: *http://www.ascilite.org.au/conferences/perth04/procs/augar.html* (accessed: 15 January 2006).

15. Lamb, B. (2004) 'Wide open spaces: Wikis, ready or not', *EDUCAUSE Review* 39(5); available at: *http://www.educause.edu/ir/library/pdf/erm0452.pdf* and *http://www.educause.edu/pub/er/erm04/erm0452.asp* (accessed: 18 February 2006).

16. Raman, M., Ryan, T. and Olfman, L. (2005). Designing knowledge management systems for teaching and learning with wiki technology. *Journal of Information Systems Education* 16(3): 311–20; available at: *http://www.findarticles.com/p/articles/mi_qa4041/is_200510/ai_n15715 725* (accessed: 15 January 2006).

17. Government of South Australia, Department of Education and Children's Services (2005) 'Learning and teaching with the Internet', *Technology School of the Future*; available at: *http://www.tsof.edu.au/projects/plict/LTI/* (accessed: 15 January 2006).

18. Lange, M. and Paterson, J. (2005) 'Using a wiki for a collaborative essay', in *An Introduction to Digital Learning Environments*, University of Edinburgh; available at: *http://revolution.lexicall.org/wiki/tiki-index.php?page= WikiWebs* and (in wiki format) at *http://www.malts.ed.ac.uk/idel/assignment/wiki/000008.html* (accessed: 15 January 2006).

19. James, H. (2004) 'My brilliant failure: Wikis in classrooms', *Kairosnews*; available at: *http://kairosnews.org/node/3794* (accessed: 15 January 2006).

20. Godwin-Jones, R. (2003) 'Blogs and wikis: Environments for on-line collaboration', *Language, Learning and Technology* 7(2): 12–16; available at: *http://llt.msu.edu/vol7num2/emerging/default.html* (accessed: 15 January 2006).

21. Bulfin, S. (2005) 'Conversation + collaboration + writing = professional learning', in B. Doecke and G. Parr (eds) *Writing = Learning*. Kent Town, South Australia: Wakefield Press/Australian Association for the Teaching of English; pp. 40–58.

22. Ibid.

23. See: *http://www.moodle.org/*.

24. Allison, P. (2005) 'High school students (and teachers) write collaboratively on a wiki'. *Weblogs & Wikis & Feeds, Oh My! Paul Allison's Reflections on Teaching and Learning in New Territories*; available at: *http://www.nycwp.org/paulallison/2005/12/04* (accessed: 15 January 2006).

25. Fountain, op. cit.

26. See: *http://www.jot.com*.

27. education.au for ACT Department of Education and Training, Canberra (2005) 'Emerging technologies: a framework for thinking'; available at: *http://www.det.act.gov.au/publicat/pdf/emergingtechnologies.pdf* (accessed: 15 January 2006).

28. See: *http://www.moodle.org*.

29. Sinofsky, S. (2005) 'Steven Sinofsky: Microsoft Professional Developers Conference 2005'; available at: *http://www.microsoft.com/presspass/exec/ssinofsky/09-14PDC2005.mspx* (accessed: 19 February 2006).

30. Schwartz, L., Clark, S., Cossarin, M. and Rudolph, J. (2004) 'Educational wikis: features and selection criteria', *International Review of Research in Open and Distance Learning* 5(1); available at: *http://www.irrodl.org/content/v5.1/technote_xxvii.html* (accessed: 18 February 2006).

31. Wang, C. and Turner, D. (2004) 'Extending the wiki paradigm for use in the classroom'. Paper presented at the *IEEE International Conference on Information Technology:*

Coding and Computing (ITCC'04); available at: *http:// doi.ieeecomputersociety.org/10.1109/ITCC.2004.1286462* (accessed: 3 January 2006).

32. Preece J. (2004) 'Etiquette online: from nice to necessary', *Communications of the ACM* 47(4): 56–61.

33. A play on 'wicketkeeper', a critical role in a cricket team. See the Wikipedia definition of *Wicket-keeper* at: *http:// en.wikipedia.org/wiki/Wicketkeeper* (page dated: 14:46, 14 February 2006; accessed: 18 February 2006).

7

Creating a wiki – the technology options

Jane Klobas and Marco Marlia

So, you've decided that you want to create a wiki. How do you go about it? There are some good technical sources in books[1] and on the Web, some of which are referred to in this chapter. Here, we present a summary of the technology options, written primarily for readers with little technical background.

Introduction to the options

Broadly speaking, there are six paths to wiki creation:

- *Path 1: Web hosting.* The simplest way to create a wiki is to open a wiki using one of the hosting services that are provided on the World Wide Web. Your wiki will be up and running in few minutes and all the technical issues will be dealt with by the service provider. Hosted services come with different subscription options (from free to 'corporate') offering different features and services. Some web hosting services offer a limited range of features and services while others offer more. If you need specific features not offered by a hosting service, or if you are not prepared to rely on an external provider, you need to pursue another path.

- *Path 2: Application service provider.* An application service provider (ASP) maintains hardware, software ('applications') and network connections at their own site on behalf of a client organisation. It is becoming increasingly common for organisations of all sizes to outsource their technical systems requirements to ASPs. A typical relationship with an ASP is based on a personally negotiated contract and service agreement.[2] If you use an ASP, you can expect them to take care of all the technical details that you specify for the wiki software that you have chosen.

- *Path 3: Appliance.* Another model that is becoming popular for organisational information systems is the appliance model. With this model, you buy hardware that is already configured with all the software, from operating system to application software, that you need to run a system. You can buy a wiki appliance as a 'black box' that is fully configured to run your wiki. The appliance will be up and running once it is configured to run in your specific network environment. You can buy and install a sophisticated system that includes many wiki features in this way.

- *Path 4: Simple installation.* You may prefer to load wiki software on your own server. Options in this path include wiki engines that are easy to install and the 'simple install' option of wiki engines that can also be used in 'advanced installation' mode. In most cases, you download the wiki software from the Web, install it and set up a few configuration details to suit your environment and needs.

This path suits individuals and groups with some technical skills, but does not need programming.

- *Path 5: Advanced installation.* Some of the popular wiki engines require installation of a number of software components, as well as configuration of the web server on which the wiki will run. This path is only suitable if you, or someone in your organisation, has the technical skills to manage a wiki implementation project. Typically, you would need a skilled network administrator or system administrator.

- *Path 6: Embedded wiki.* Wiki capability is being embedded in other types of software. This is particularly common with learning management systems such as the popular open source Moodle.[3] Embedded wikis have all the basic features of wikis, but they do not generally have as wide a range of features as purpose-specific wiki systems. We will not consider this path in detail in this chapter because the primary choice is that of the software in which the wiki is embedded, rather than the wiki itself. Nonetheless, the information about wiki functioning and features in this chapter will help if you need to evaluate embedded wikis.

One fundamental choice is between a hosted path (paths 1 and 2) and installation on your own premises (paths 3–5). Paths 1 and 2 offer the advantages that you will be up and running quickly, you incur no hardware costs, and maintenance costs are usually limited to any fees that you pay for the service. Paths 3–5 offer the advantage of greater control as you will be using your own resources. Paths 4 and 5 also offer the advantage that you have control over your wiki installation.

How wikis work

Conceptually, wikis have four basic elements:

- *The content*, created by users and stored on the server. The content is usually stored as marked-up text, where the marks indicate how the text will be displayed when the content appears in a browser (e.g. text stored as *markup language* might be displayed in bold: **markup language**). As we noted in Chapter 1, some wikis also allow images, mathematical formulae and attachments, while others can include calls to software routines that enhance the wiki's functionality or allow access to other applications from within the wiki.

- *The template*, which defines the layout of pages in the wiki, including the standard information to be included on each page, such as the header and footer, a logo, the edit and revision buttons, and page revision number or date.

- *The wiki engine*, the software – written in a programming language such as PHP, Perl or Java – that handles all the 'business logic' of the wiki. For example, when a user requests display of a wiki page, the wiki engine generates a wiki page that displays the content of the requested page using the template (see Figure 7.1). The wiki engine enables all types of page that users see in a wiki, including content, revision and editing pages, to be displayed. It also accepts instructions to save an edited page, saves new or changed content to the server, manages user access rights and executes instructions for other wiki features.

- *The wiki page*, which is created by the wiki engine from the content and the template, when a user requests that a page be displayed in their browser.

Figure 7.1 Wiki engines draw content from the database and layout from the template file to display a wiki page in a web browser

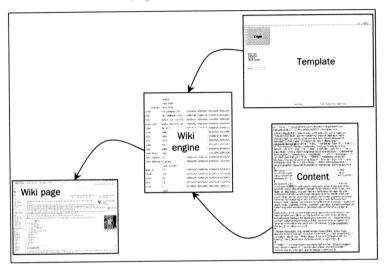

How wiki engines differ

Wiki engines differ in a number of ways:

- the features offered;
- the ways in which each feature is implemented;
- the way in which the content is stored;
- the type of licence that is required to run the software;
- the platform (hardware, operating system and other software) required to run the software.

Wiki features

In Chapter 1, we introduced the basic features of most wikis: collaborative authorship, simple editing, quick updating, ability to add pages simply and quickly, ability to track changes and view recent changes, and a simple permissions structure to manage reading, authoring and administration privileges. Additional features are offered by most wiki engines. An extensive list of features and differences in their implementation in different wiki engines, is available at the WikiMatrix wiki comparison site.[4] Some of these features are introduced here:

- *Language support.* This may be an important feature for wikis that are used in an international context. Most wiki engines support Unicode which allows the writing of non-Latin characters and some support right-to-left writing as well as left-to-right.

- *Media and file support.* Many wikis allow images to be included in the wiki page and some even allow videos and other media to be embedded in pages. Some also allow files to be attached. Advanced wikis allow versioning and commenting on attached files, and some are able to search the full text of attachments.

- *Mathematical notation.* Some wikis specifically support mathematical notation and formulae.

- *Conflict handling.* When two people edit the same page at the same time an editing conflict may occur. Some wiki engines simply ignore the conflict, which means the person who saves the page last overwrites all changes made by the first person. Other wiki engines notify the second editor of the possible conflict. Another group of solutions locks pages to avoid conflicts. The lock usually has a time limit to avoid pages being locked indefinitely when the connection or browser crashes. Another approach, as yet rarely employed, is to show colliding text in real time while people are editing the same page.

- *Spam handling.* One way to reduce spam in editable websites such as wikis and blogs is to introduce a captcha test to confirm that an instruction has been issued by a human rather than a computer program or bot. Most captcha tests consist of an image containing some distorted letters or numbers. The user must read and enter these letters and numbers when sending their details or saving a page. Spam is avoided because software cannot respond to the captcha test and thus cannot submit data or save a page. Visual captcha tests cannot be used by some visually impaired people, but other captcha tests are available.[5] As spam becomes more of a problem, wiki engines are developing automated techniques for identifying and filtering out spam.

- *News feeds.* In Chapter 1, we mentioned news aggregators as tools for alerting users to changes in wikis. Some wikis have also introduced the use of feeders in the other direction, to aggregate content from other sources (online portals, other wikis) into the wiki.

- *Style sheets.* Recall that wiki engines display contents according to the template (Figure 7.1). Many wiki systems come with standard templates in a number of different styles (they tend to differ in terms of colour and font rather than basic layout). While some wiki engines assist with development of a template style of your own design, most of these are constrained by the basic template that reflects the functionality of the specific wiki engine.

- *E-mail integration.* In Chapter 1, we also mentioned that e-mail can be used as an alerting tool. Some wikis also permit content to be added to the wiki by e-mail and some allow a page to be sent to one or more e-mail addresses.

■ *Integration with other social software tools.* Some wikis provide integration with other social software tools such as weblogs, polls that allow users to vote for a choice, shared whiteboards and mind-mapping software. The seedwiki and Confluence wiki engines permit users to add labels (also known as tags) to pages, giving these engines the capability to act as social classification software. Just as in social classification software, it is possible to map the 'tag space' to get an idea of the topics currently under discussion in the wiki. As Figure 7.2 shows, the more popular the topic, the larger the font. Clicking on the topic produces a linked list of pages that have used the tag.

■ *Plugins and extensions.* Many wikis enable the basic features to be extended with custom plugins. Even for proprietary software, the plugins and extensions are often open source.[6] Wikis with an active community often have extensive sets of plugins and extensions.

Figure 7.2   A display of popular labels within a Confluence wiki

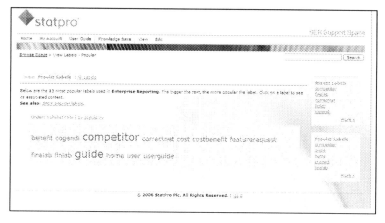

- *Number of wikis.* Some wiki engines and hosting services support only one wiki while others support multiple wikis.

- *Export and back-up.* Several wiki engines offer a number of options for export of the wiki in formats that include HTML, XML and PDF. A small number of wiki engines offer the possibility of backing up the wiki itself, while most rely on back-up of the entire server on which the wiki resides.

Implementation of features

Even when wikis share the same feature, the feature is often implemented differently. We consider some of the common differences here:

- *Security.* Different wikis offer different options for control of access to the wiki and wiki pages. Some wikis assume that the wiki will be open to all to read and write and offer no access security features, while others provide the ability to control read, write and editing (e.g. page removal or reversion) access for each wiki, wiki section and wiki page. The most sophisticated can be integrated with an organisation's existing Lightweight Directory Access Protocol (LDAP) databases to identify users and groups.[7]

- *Editing syntax.* While almost every wiki system has a markup (formatting) language, and these languages or syntaxes all have some elements in common, different wiki engines have implemented different syntaxes over time. However, the differences in markup language are not so great that markup language should constitute a reason for choosing one wiki engine over another. More important is the difference between use of a markup language and WYSIWYG editing. WYSIWYG editors (also known as Rich Text Editors) enable authors to write much as they do when they prepare a simple word processed document. Simple WYSIWYG editors have some disadvantages; for example, older versions of browsers do not support WYSIWYG editing, so additional time may be required to load the editing page because the WYSIWYG functionality needs also to be added. In addition, there remain some 'glitches' in some WYSIWYG implementations so that the displayed page may not always match the edited page. Some members of the wiki community believe that WYSIWYG editing distracts from the wiki principle that the text is simple; however, wiki users who are familiar with word processing, but not with the use of markup languages, may in fact find WYSIWYG less distracting and more satisfying than marking up text. Some wikis enable the user to choose between using markup language and WYSIWYG editing.

- *Editing individual sections of a page.* Some wiki engines enable the text on a page to be divided into sections. Wikis built with these wiki engines provide an edit button for each section of text.

- *Adding links.* One of the 'quick' features of wikis is that links are simply included in the text as an author is writing. Many wiki engines use the syntax feature called CamelCase to identify a link: any word that combines upper and lower case letters creates a link to a page – if the page does not already exist within the wiki, a new page is flagged with the name provided in CamelCase. Others (notably MediaWiki, which drives Wikipedia) require links to be marked up in the same way as other features of the text. The wiki community has passionate arguments for and against CamelCase, but the only difference we can see, once a user is familiar with the syntax used in a particular wiki, is that CamelCase will create links, even when they are not wanted, such as for names like McKenzie. These 'false links' can, however, be quickly undone with a click or a keystroke. Some wikis allow both approaches.

- *Change alerts.* News feeds enable editors, authors and users to request notification of changes. Depending on the depth of implementation of feed aggregators in the wiki software, feeds might be added to existing wiki pages and be used to notify of new page creation, new comments and changes to user profile information. Some wikis provide e-mail notification of changes to the wiki or specific pages or sections of it in addition to, or in place of, news feeds.

- *Search.* As most wikis save content in a rather unstructured way, a search feature is critical. In some wiki engines you can search page titles only, while others provide full-text search. The quality of the search results displays varies considerably, but most are poor. The majority of wiki engines simply produce a list of page titles, without any reference to the search word or its context (unless it happens to appear in the title). Many of the lists are in alphabetical order. MediaWiki estimates and produces a list in order of percentage relevancy. Confluence provides two lines that place the search term(s) in context. The search feature becomes more useful but more resource-intensive the more content is indexed, so full-text searches put more pressure on the server than searches that are limited to titles. Some wiki engines use cookies or other techniques to limit the number of queries from a user, while others reduce search time using memory caching features. If search is important for your application, you should pay close attention to the search features, limitations and, if you are installing the wiki yourself, any special technical requirements to support searches.

Storage of contents

Some wikis store each page as a file while others use relational database management systems (RDBMS) such as MySQL. Most wikis store not just the current version of the content, but earlier versions as well.

Licensing

There are both proprietary (or 'commercial') and open source wiki engines. In both cases, the source code may be made available to the user. In the case of open source wiki engines the source code is free and public, while it can only be obtained with a licence (which may require payment) from a proprietary provider. In practical terms, ownership of the source code is only useful if you plan to modify the wiki engine in some way or do some in-house programming to integrate existing systems with the wiki, but plugins and extensions exist for both proprietary and open source wiki engines, so it may be possible to use a tool that has already been written rather than write one yourself.

The majority of wiki engines are open source. Most are issued under a GNU General Public License (GPL)[8] which gives users the freedom to share and change the software, but not to incorporate it in a commercial product or system. If you need to incorporate your wiki in commercial software, look for a wiki engine released under a licence that permits this.

If you opt for open source software, you are responsible for all installation, configuration and maintenance. The popular open source wiki engines have strong communities that provide support (through discussion lists and sometimes personal e-mail) for these processes, but adoption of open source usually requires some technical skills and staff time. Commercial support is also available for some of the larger open source wiki engines. Proprietary systems offer services for installation, configuration and maintenance. The popular proprietary systems also have active support and development communities. While relying on community support has its advantages, you should be aware of two issues associated with community support. Software support communities often conduct quite technical discussions, so it is a good idea to get an idea of the community before you choose a wiki engine. Remember, too, that if something goes wrong with your wiki installation and you are relying on community support, you may not get an immediate reply to your query and may have to wait before you can fix the problem.

The choice of proprietary or open source comes down to your attitude to proprietary software, your own or your organisation's technical skills and where you assign your costs. Wikis were originally associated with the open source software movement and many wiki founders will only consider open source software. The majority of open source engines require advanced installation and maintenance, so if you have limited technical skills, these wiki engines are not suitable for your needs. There may actually be little difference in the total costs of using proprietary and open source software. The cost of open source software is primarily the indirect cost of staff time. The costs of proprietary software are direct, primarily the cost of purchasing the software licence and services that you need.

Some proprietary software providers provide free licences for individual and not-for-profit organisations; in this case, the purchase price of proprietary and open source software is the same (zero) and the cost of support may even be similar, especially if support is provided primarily by the community of users of the wiki engine.

Wiki platform

The technical platform required for installation of a wiki includes the hardware (the computer), the operating system, web server software, software required to support the programming language in which the wiki engine is written, and database management system if your wiki engine uses a database.

You will need a computer that is capable of running the wiki software. In most cases, this means you will need a computer already configured as a web server, but some wiki engines also come with web server software and so can run on most computers, including an individual's PC. You will also need to make sure your computer has enough space for your wiki and enough RAM (the memory used during processing) to run the wiki engine that you select. (Some technical details: MediaWiki, for example, requires about 5–10 MB per process to start up and up to 50 MB per thread for certain operations.)

Most wiki engines, like other web-based applications, are multi-platform, i.e. they are developed to run on many operating systems. Over time, wiki engines have appeared in several programming languages. The WikiWikiWeb list of wiki engines, described as the 'canonical list' of wiki engines includes wikis in a dozen different programming languages.[9] There is even a wiki engine developed using Microsoft Word macros.

If you want to make modifications to your wiki software, or want to use open source plugins and extensions to proprietary software, you should choose a wiki engine that is written in a language with which you are familiar. If your wiki uses a relational database, you need to be sure that you also have an appropriate RDBMS on your web server. Depending on the software and whether you intend to make modifications, you may also need some expertise in management of the RDBMS. It is also worth confirming that the wiki engine you choose is suitable for the browsers that your users will be using.

Choosing a wiki path

Having examined how wikis differ from one another, we are in a position to examine the options in more detail. Here are some questions that can help to understand your needs and constraints.

- Will it be a mission critical wiki, a small group activity, or a trial or for fun? Will you need to integrate the wiki with other organisational systems? If you just want to see how wikis work or to create a short-term wiki for a small group, you might want to start with a hosted wiki.

- Do you or your organisation have access to the technical skills available to install and maintain a wiki on your own server? If not, you should use a wiki hosting service or employ an ASP to set up and maintain the wiki technology for you.

- What features do you need? Want? Want to avoid? These questions will guide your choice of a specific wiki engine:

  - Do you want just one or many wikis?

- Do you need a specific character set or alphabet support?

- Do you need support for images, mathematical expressions, attachments or other media?

- How many users are you anticipating? How many of these will be readers, authors, or editors with special privileges? Do you need specific user management, permissions and authorisation, or other security features?

- How large will the wiki be? How important is the search engine? If it is important, what features do you need?

- Do you have preferences for any of the other features mentioned in this chapter or at WikiMatrix?[10]

■ Does your budget support direct payment for software and services, or must all costs be indirect costs? If all costs must be indirect and you are an organisation other than a not-for-profit organisation, your choice will be restricted to free hosting services and open source wiki engines.

■ Do you have technical constraints (e.g. operating system, browser compatibility needs, RDBMS availability)?

Armed with these questions, we can now examine in more detail the options in each of the five main paths (paths 1–5) that we identified at the beginning of the chapter. The paths are summarised in Figure 7.3, which compares them along the two axes defined by the first two questions: need for reliability and integration, and available IT skills.

Figure 7.3 The chosen path for creating a wiki depends on need for reliability and complexity and available IT skills

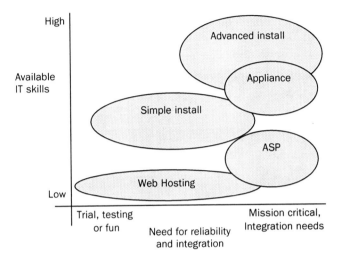

Web hosting

Wikis can be hosted on both proprietary and open source platforms and there are quite a few wiki hosting services to choose from. Some issues to take into account when you choose a hosting service are the subscription costs, features available at each subscription level, technical reliability (e.g. in terms of uptime), customer support and continuity. Some hosting services offer you the option of establishing your own domain name, while others offer you only a domain name within their own site; this can be an important issue if you want to create a personalised image for your wiki. Ease of setup might also be an issue, but almost all of the wiki hosting services enable you to set up a wiki with a few clicks.

Continuity is an issue with hosting of any kind of information service, not just wikis. When your wiki is hosted by an external provider, you want to be sure that the provider will continue to be 'in business' for as long as you need your wiki. Hosting services with active communities or large user bases are the most likely to continue. To be sure that your wiki is secure, you should develop a back-up strategy.

Some of the most popular wiki hosting services are reviewed here. Socialtext, which also acts as a host, is reviewed in the section on appliances. An annotated list of wiki hosting services is available from Wikibooks[11] and an introduction and a brief comparison is available on Wikipedia.[12] More information about finding wiki hosting services is given at the end of this chapter.

Seedwiki

www.seedwiki.com

Seedwiki is a popular hosting service. With a free account, you can start any number of wikis or blogs and have unlimited pages. Many languages, including languages that use non-roman scripts, are supported. There are no advertisements on seedwiki, but all wikis developed with the free account are available on the public Web. Paid plans range from US$10–$50 per month and offer password protection along with other functions. The most expensive plan lets you create your own 'wiki farm' which you can set up to appear to be separate from seedwiki. Wikis created in seedwiki have the simple look and feel of more 'traditional' wikis. They offer WYSIWYG editing.

Wikia

http://www.wikias.org

Wikia (formerly known as Wikicities) is a community-oriented wiki hosting site. All Wikia are hosted for free and offer the full functionality of the MediaWiki wiki engine (the wiki engine that powers Wikipedia) including multiple language support, RSS feeds and the ability to include images and other files. Like Wikipedia, all wikis are openly editable and the text is available under the GNU Free Documentation License. Focused on community development, users of Wikia sites have full access to free technical and social support for their wiki. Wikia manages some of the Internet's largest wikis outside of Wikipedia, including Memory Alpha, the Star Trek encyclopaedia and Wookieepedia, the Star Wars wiki. Wikia has a strong and active community base.

JotSpot

http://www.jotspot.com

JotSpot is a commercial wiki hosting service. JotSpot will host a small, private wiki for up to four users and 20 pages for free. Larger paid plans range from US$9.95 per month for ten users and 100 pages to the company plan at $199.95 per month. Paid plans include the ability to publish the wiki to the Web and to control access at the individual user level. The larger plans offer unlimited users and large or unlimited page limits and the ability to use your own domain. JotSpot's features include WYSIWYG editing, an 'application gallery' of wiki page styles pre-formatted to support such activities as blogging; maintaining a company directory, contact list or call log; and the ability to write customised applications to extend wiki functioning.

Application service providers

Many organisation act as ASPs. Some may be prepared to host all your organisational systems, not just your wiki. Some ASPs will host the wiki engine of your choice, even if they have not had past experience with it. There are also some specialist wiki ASPs. Some of these specialise in one wiki engine only, while others will host the wiki engine of your choice. Socialtext acts as an ASP for its own proprietary software. A UK-based company, Adaptavist, is an ASP dedicated to the proprietary Confluence wiki engine, and acts for organisations throughout the world.[13]

Wiki appliances

Two commercial providers, Socialtext and JotSpot, offer a wiki appliance option. Contact JotSpot directly for information about their JotBox appliance. A picture and details of the current configurations of the Socialtext appliance, are available on the Socialtext website.[14] After initial configuration by the provider, it may be possible for some local configuration to be done, such as setting the frequency of e-mail notifications. Appliances come with standard wiki templates and designs. If you want assistance to customise the design for your own organisation, you need to pay for this service.

Socialtext

http://www.socialtext.com

Socialtext provides wikis geared towards workgroups and enterprises, available as a hosted service or a behind-the-firewall appliance. Socialtext is stable, easy to use and scales well to large installations. The code is mostly proprietary, written in Perl and Javascript. The hosted service is free for up to five users with unlimited wikis and for open source projects. There is a private community of customers who share practices and tips and make suggestions. Socialtext is moving toward more open source code and building a developer community to support this move.

Simple installation

There are both proprietary and open source options for simple installation of wiki software on your own server. We provide examples of one popular proprietary wiki engine and three well-known open source wiki engines here. For an up-to-date list of wiki engines for simple installation, go to WikiWikiWeb's Wiki Choice Tree.[15]

Confluence

http://atlassian.com/software/confluence/

- *Programming language*: Java;
- *Licence*: commercial (free for non-profit, open source or personal use and half-price educational licences);
- *Stability*: enterprise-grade stability;
- *User base*: 1000+ organisations in 60+ countries;
- *Community*: very active;
- *Description*: extremely flexible wiki;
- *Pros*: easy to use, large library of stable open source plugins, fast; includes full version control, printable templates, themes, content templates, enterprise-grade security, mail archiving, news, comments, powerful search engine, automated backups, file attachments, extensive navigation features (site map, alphabetical index, recently updated pages, etc.), content labelling, export content to XML, PDF and Word, text formatting and much more, LDAP support, scalable to large installations;

- *Cons*: currently no content approval process;
- *Notes*: Confluence (also known as Atlassian Confluence) is a widely used proprietary wiki engine which can be installed in simple and advanced modes. It has an active development and support community. Wikis and websites created with Confluence have an attractive look and feel.

UseModWiki

http://www.usemod.com/cgi-bin/wiki.pl

- *Programming language*: Perl;
- *Licence*: GPL;
- *Stability*: high;
- *Community*: medium;
- *Description*: 'UseModWiki is an implementation of the original Wiki concept created by Ward Cunningham';
- *Pros*: stable, Unicode support, conflict detection;
- *Cons*: content stored in files with no database support, very plain user interface, no advanced editing, poor display of search results;
- *Notes*: UseMod has probably been overtaken by other wiki engines ('WikiClones'), but it is interesting if you want to see how the original wiki concept was implemented.

PmWiki

http://www.pmwiki.org

- *Programming language*: PHP;
- *Licence*: GPL;

- *Stability*: good;

- *Community*: medium;

- *Description*: 'PmWiki is a wiki-based system for collaborative creation and maintenance of websites';

- *Pros*: good plugin architecture, sidebar assists with navigation;

- *Cons*: content stored in files, but database support is available with a plugin;

- *Notes*: comparable in many ways with UseModWiki. It has many more native features than UseModWiki, but heavy reliance on plugins for other features means that it is really only easy to install if you are prepared to accept the less feature-rich base version.

PhpWiki

http://phpwiki.sourceforge.net

- *Programming language*: PHP;

- *Licence*: GPL;

- *Stability*: high;

- *Community*: small;

- *Description*: 'PhpWiki is a Php clone of the original WikiWikiWeb';

- *Pros*: easy configuration, supports many databases, powerful plugin and list syntax, full PHP in templates;

- *Cons*: not an active community, no Unicode support;

- *Notes*: PhpWiki needs only to be downloaded and unpacked. No configuration is required and it comes with a set of default pages.

Advanced installation

Some well-known wiki engines require more advanced skills. In this section, we review the advanced installation wiki engines behind many of the wikis included in this book. There are many other available wiki engines. If there is a specific feature that you must implement, you can find guidance at WikiWikiWeb's Wiki Choice Tree.[16] If you need a bundle of features, the decision support system at WikiMatrix can help identify those wiki engines that support your needs.[17]

MediaWiki

http://www.mediawiki.org

- *Programming language*: PHP;
- *Licence*: GPL;
- *Stability*: very high;
- *Community*: very active;
- *Description*: 'MediaWiki is a free software package originally written for Wikipedia';
- *Pros*: supports high traffic, very stable, many features, data stored in a database, offers caching;
- *Cons*: configuration process requires technical expertise;
- *Notes*: MediaWiki appears to be the most popular of the open source wiki engines. Its success as the engine behind Wikipedia has much to do with that, but its rich set of features and ability to reliably support high traffic wikis across multiple servers also make it popular. MediaWiki can be complicated to configure. If your technical skills are limited, it may be better to use a MediaWiki-based hosting service such as Wikia.

MoinMoin

http://moinmoin.wikiwikiweb.de

- *Programming language*: Python;
- *Licence:* GPL;
- *Stability*: high;
- *Community*: very active;
- *Description*: 'MoinMoin is an advanced, easy to use and extensible WikiEngine with a large community of users';
- *Pros*: fast, easy to use;
- *Cons*: requires Python support, data stored on files;
- *Notes*: MoinMoin is easy to use, fast and modular. It has a large community of users and because Python is a simple programming language, it also has lots of people writing extensions for it. The name is a common German slang expression.

TikiWiki

http://tikiwiki.org

- *Programming language*: PHP;
- *Licence:* LGPL;
- *Stability*: high;
- *Community*: very active;
- *Description*: 'Tikiwiki is a full featured Free Software ... Wiki/CMS/Groupware written in PHP';
- *Pros*: versatile content management, many features, supports many databases, international community, Unicode support;

- *Cons*: no WYSIWYG;
- *Notes*: TikiWiki is a popular wiki with a large and active international community.

TWiki

http://twiki.org

- *Programming language*: Perl;
- *Licence*: GPL;
- *Stability*: high;
- *Community*: medium;
- *Description*: 'web-based collaboration platform targeting the corporate intranet world';
- *Pros*: feature rich, easy to use, groupware oriented, many plugins;
- *Cons*: file based;
- *Notes*: TWiki differs from the other wikis in this list in its emphasis on corporate applications, typically project work, document management and knowledge management. Users listed in TWiki documentation include British Telecom, Disney, SAP and Yahoo!

WikiD

http://www.oclc.org/research/projects/wikid/default.htm

- *Programming language*: Java;
- *Licence*: Apache;
- *Stability*: moderate;
- *Community*: small;

- *Description*: WikiD extends the wiki model to include multiple data collections using any XML Schema;

- *Pros*: extremely configurable and extensible (XSL and Java abstractions); arbitrary record formats (MARC, METS, Dublin Core, etc); lightweight, standards-based APIs (OpenURL, SRU, OAI, RSS, etc.);

- *Cons*: customisation process not for users without technical skills;

- *Notes*: WikiD is a specific extension of the wiki model for digital libraries. Wikis are generally limited to a single collection containing a single kind of record. WikiD (Wiki/Data) extends the Wiki model to support multiple WikiCollections containing arbitrary schemas of XML records with minimal additional complexity.

Finding and comparing wiki hosting services and engines

Hosting services

A number of directories are available to help with searches for wiki hosting services. The directories include services that host both public and private wikis. Some of these directories are wikis so they allow providers and users of hosting services to list the service in the directory and to write (or amend) the description of it. (Wiki hosting services are also known as 'wiki farms' in the jargon adopted by the wiki development community.) To find a wiki hosting service that uses a particular platform, you can use your favourite search engine to search for the word *hosting* with the name of the wiki engine.

Google Wiki Farms Directory

http://directory.google.com/Top/Computers/Software/Groupware/ Wiki/Wiki_Farms/

Most of the major wiki hosting services are listed in the Google 'wiki farms' directory. The directory provides links to the homepages of each of the hosting services followed by a 1–2 line description of features and services.

Wiki Farms

http://c2.com/cgi/wiki? WikiFarms

This wiki, on WikiWikiWeb, lists a large number of wiki hosting services, from the well-known to the obscure. The services are classified as free or commercial. Free wiki hosting services are distinguished by language (English and not English). The free English language services are further rated as four star or three or fewer stars. The commercial services are listed in order of price per month of hosting. The contributors to this wiki include brief notes with the link to each hosting service. The notes vary but may include information about whether the service is considered active or reliable, the features of the hosting service and the wiki engine or software that underlies it. Some of the listed hosting services also have separate WikiWikiWeb entries that contain more information.

List of Wiki Farms

http://en.wikipedia.org/wiki/List_of_wiki_farms

Wikipedia contains a list of wiki hosting services. The list is in the form of a table that includes the name of the hosting service, whether it is free or payment is required and the wiki engine that underlies it. In some cases, there is a very brief overview of the hosting service's features. Some entries also include information about the content licences that are expected to be honoured by hosted wikis.

Free Hosted Wikis: Comparison of Wiki Farms

http://pascal.vanhecke.info/2005/10/30/free-hosted-wikis-comparison-of-wiki-farms/

Pascal Van Hecke recorded his findings as he searched for a place to host a wiki 'to collect ideas for the programme [of an event], keep track of task lists and let people subscribe for the event (by simply adding names)'. This page from his blog includes concise notes and an evaluation of each of the wiki hosting services he considered.

e-Learning Centre: Wiki Tools

http://www.e-learningcentre.co.uk/eclipse/vendors/wikis.htm

The UK e-Learning Centre maintains a list of 'wiki tools' that includes both wiki hosting services and wiki engines or software to download. The directory includes new products on the market as well as some of the more established wiki platforms. It is well laid out and includes a concise and useful review of each listed tool.

Wiki Hosting Services

http://www.davidmattison.ca/tiki/tiki-index.php?page_ref_id=40

This short list, on David Mattison's site, included, at the time of writing, some hosting services that were not included in the other directories.

Finding wiki engines

The most effective way to find wiki software is through directories. Some directories also provide comparisons.

WikiMatrix

http://www.wikimatrix.org

WikiMatrix allows you to select and compare wiki engines and hosting services based on their features. There were 46 wiki engines in the list at the time of writing. There is a brief summary of each of the wiki engines (the information may have been provided by the owner or author of the wiki engine) accompanied by some screen shots. If you know which wiki engines or hosting services you would like to compare, select them and ask for a comparison. WikiMatrix produces a table with a feature by feature comparison (at the time of writing, comparisons were based on 111 features and characteristics) and, where applicable, a comparison of the markup languages used for editing. Alternatively, you can use the 'Wiki Choice Wizard' to produce a list of wikis that meet your needs based on your answers to a series of questions that the wizard asks. This is an extremely useful site. WikiMatrix is not, however, a wiki so it may not always be as up to date as the wiki-based directories whose entries are added by the wiki engine sponsors and distributors themselves.

Wiki Choicetree

http://c2.com/cgi/wiki?WikiChoicetree

The WikiWikiWeb wiki choicetree lists wiki engines by feature. The features are: data stored in flat/text file (no database necessary), SQL database support, Unicode support, Wikipedia-style markup, user permissions (entries in this section are annotated to indicate the types of permission supported), cascading style sheets, quick change (without needing to edit page), fully functional on portable devices, super easy installation on hosted servers, RSS feed syndication, subscription for e-mail notification of recent changes, send e-mail in to the wiki, wiki whiteboard, visual editing, version control, plugins architecture, editing individual sections of a page, categories, search, content upload, attachments, polls and votes, spreadsheet calculations, charts and graphs, web-based presentations, mind map support and more.

Google

http://directory.google.com/Top/Computers/Software/ Groupware/Wiki/Wiki_Engines/

The Google directory of wiki engines is substantial. Each link is followed by a brief description. Most descriptions include the main features supported by the wiki engine and some include basic technical information. Many of the wiki engines are also classified by the programming language in which they are written (Java, Perl, PHP, Python, etc.).

Wikipedia List of Wiki Software

http://en.wikipedia.org/wiki/List_of_wiki_software

Wikipedia provides a longer list of wiki engines, classified by underlying programming language. Most entries include brief, mostly technical, descriptions of the wiki software.

Wikipedia Comparison of Wiki Software

http://en.wikipedia.org/wiki/Comparison_of_wiki_software

Wikipedia also contains a comparison table. Although fewer wiki engines are included in this table than in WikiMatrix, the details available for comparison are different. They include release information, target audience, details of the technical platform (operating system and other software required) for installation and a note on ease of installation.

MoinMoin WikiEngineComparison

http://moinmoin.wikiwikiweb.de/WikiEngineComparison

Another comparison table, comparing just over a dozen wikis, but includes a couple of criteria that are not included at the other comparison sites.

Long List of Wiki Clones

http://c2.com/w4/wikibase/?LongListOfWikiClones

Technical wiki aficionados still value this now rather aged (November 2003) list of wiki engines. Most entries include the URL of the site from which the software can be accessed, the name of the author, the name or names of earlier wiki engines on which the software is based (hence the title word 'clones') and some technical information about additional software needed to run the wiki engine. Some entries also include an overview of the technical features of the software and the available documentation.

Future of wiki software

The future of wiki software is strongly tied with the evolution of the Internet. As wikis are still quite new, both as technology and as collaboration paradigm, we can expect improvements in maturity and stability of the software and standardisation of the features and interfaces. Not all the wiki engines that are available now will continue to be supported and new wiki engines will appear.

Notes

1. Leuf, B. and Cunningham, W. (2001) *The Wiki Way: Quick Collaboration on the Web*. Boston: Addison-Wesley; Ebersbach, A., Glaser, M. and Heigl, R. (2006) *Wiki: Web Collaboration*. Berlin, Heidelberg: Springer.
2. An excellent introduction to ASPs appears in Kancheva, E. (2002) 'Application service providers: an alternative model for IT services delivery', *EDUCAUSE Research Bulletin*, 14 May; ERB0210; available at: *http://www.educause.edu/LibraryDetailPage/666?ID=ERB0210* (accessed: 20 February 2006).
3. See: *http://www.moodle.org*.
4. See: *http://www.wikimatrix.org*.
5. Wikipedia (2006) 'Captcha'; available at: *http://en.wikipedia.org/wiki/Captcha* (page dated 17:20, 16 February 2006; accessed: 19 February 2006).
6. The homepages for wiki engines that support plugins and extensions provide a link to them. To get an idea of how many ways plugins and extensions might be used, see: Atlassian (2006) 'Confluence extensions home'; available at: *http://confluence.atlassian.com/display/CONFEXT* (page dated 16 February 2006; accessed: 20 February 2006).
7. For more information about LDAP, see the Wikipedia definition at: *http://en.wikipedia.org/wiki/LDAP* (page dated 01:52, 17 February 2006; accessed: 20 February 2006).
8. See: *http://www.gnu.org/copyleft/gpl.html*.
9. WikiWikiWeb (2006) 'Wiki engines'; available at: *http://c2.com/cgi/wiki?WikiEngines* (page dated 18 February 2006; accessed: 20 February 2006).
10. See: *http://www.wikimatrix.org*.

11. See: *http://en.wikibooks.org/wiki/Wiki_Science:How_to_start_a_Wiki*.

12. Wikipedia (2006) 'Comparison of wiki farms'; available at: *http://en.wikipedia.org/wiki/List_of_wiki_farms* (page dated 20:20, 17 February 2006; accessed: 20 February 2006).

13. See: *www.adaptavist.com*.

14. Socialtext, 'Socialtext appliance'; available at: *http://www.socialtext.com/products/appliance/* (accessed: 20 February 2006).

15. See: *http://c2.com/cgi/wiki?WikiChoicetree*.

16. Ibid.

17. See: *http://www.wikimatrix.org*.

8

Managing a wiki

Jane Klobas and Angela Beesley

> Properly used, [wikis] can free up collaboration and
> increase employee engagement. Improperly used, they
> are neither worse nor better than any other
> collaborative technology out there. (Espen Anderson) [1]

Since 1995, a multitude of uses have been found for the
technology and procedures of wikis, but there is little
documentation about how they should be managed.[2] Yet, as
setting up a wiki or buying a hosted service is so easy, there
is a danger that wikis are created without regard for
management issues. Simply creating a wiki and expecting it
to solve a problem is not enough to achieve the goals for
which the wiki was created. The wiki will only be successful
if it is managed in such a way that it is a useful tool for the
people who will be using it.

Wiki management involves technology management,
content management and social management of wiki
contributors though policies or behavioural norms. All of
these aspects of wiki management need to be considered
throughout the life of the wiki. The management issues range
from determining the aims of the wiki in the early stages,
through technical setup and content creation, to maintenance
and evaluation of the wiki. We can imagine a wiki lifecycle
with four interrelated stages (illustrated in Figure 8.1): plan,

Figure 8.1 The wiki management lifecycle

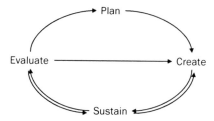

create, sustain, and evaluate. Each of these stages, and the relationships between them, will be discussed in this chapter.

Planning the wiki

A number of issues need to be considered during the planning phase: the purpose of the wiki, who it is for and the resources available for creating and maintaining it. Decisions need to be made about who will have access to the wiki and whether any limitations will be placed on editing. The wiki software needs to be chosen. In larger wikis, a decision will have to be made about whether a categorisation scheme or a system of tagging or labelling pages will improve access to wiki contents. Roles (including wiki administration and management) need to be determined and access controls set. Policies and practices for the wiki will need to be determined and documented. Decisions about the technical features of the wiki need to be made.

The purpose of the wiki

Making decisions about the purpose of the wiki, and communicating the purpose to the wiki's users, along with identifying the 'audience' for the wiki, are crucial first steps in planning a wiki. Attention to purpose and audience requires a sort of 'needs analysis' in which you test your idea of establishing a wiki against what might already be available to meet a similar purpose with a similar audience. If you can establish a unique purpose and identify an audience, you are on your way to establishing a wiki. A mission statement, containing your vision of what the wiki will be, will help readers know what to expect and keep contributors on-topic.

Resources for creating and maintaining the wiki

The nature of the wiki that you can create and maintain depends not only on its purpose and audience, but also on the available resources (and constraints on those resources). The available funds, time, hardware and software, and wiki administration, design and technical skills will all influence the nature of the wiki.

Financial resources

What is your budget for the wiki? Are any funds available, or must the wiki be managed without any direct expenditure?

If no direct costs can be incurred, you will need to build the wiki using free services or software. If you are in a category that qualifies for free hosting or free proprietary software, you have a wide variety of choice from the paths described in Chapter 7. Otherwise, your choice will involve open source software, and you will need to create and maintain the wiki using your own time and skills or those of other people in your organisation. Choose software that has a strong user support community if you have no budget to pay for support.

If a small budget is available, you can consider wiki hosting options for creating the wiki and running the software, but all other aspects of wiki management will rely on the time and skills available to you.

With larger budgets, your options increase. In addition to open source options, you might consider a commercial hosting service, using an application service provider (ASP) or buying a wiki appliance or proprietary wiki software. Even if you do not use a hosting service or ASP, you might consider outsourcing some of the technical aspects of creating and maintaining the wiki. A larger budget might also support the employment of staff to develop the visual design and information architecture of the wiki, and a wiki administrator to manage a wiki or a family of wikis throughout their life.

Time

Wiki management takes time. Even if you are able to rely on others to get the technical issues right, you will need to devote time to the information architecture and, if you want a customised look, the visual appearance of the wiki when you first create it (unless you have a separate budget for these tasks). You will need to add initial content, let people know about the wiki, provide training or user documentation, and encourage initial contributions to the wiki. Once the wiki has been created, time is needed to monitor the content and other aspects of the wiki. If your goal is to build a community, you will need to spend time on community development and support.

Technology

In Chapter 7, we mentioned some of the technology resources that are needed if you decide to run the wiki software in-house. Specifically, unless you purchase a wiki appliance, you will need to make sure that you have a computer that will support your wiki and the wiki engine that you plan to use. You may require a computer already configured as a web server. You may require a specific database management system. If you plan to modify the software, you will need access to the programming language in which the wiki is written. The amount of disk space available for storage of wiki content files needs to be sufficient for your wiki. Some wikis use a lot of RAM; check that your web server has sufficient RAM for your needs. You also need to check that the reliability and bandwidth of your network connection is appropriate for the frequency of use and type of content that your wiki contains. Finally, you need to plan how you will backup your wiki and what you will do if your wiki goes offline for any reason.

Skills

Depending on the options chosen, various skills will be needed to manage your wiki. These might include:

- planning;
- web manager;
- programming;
- visual design;
- information architect;
- content writing;
- documentation and policy writing;
- wiki content and user administration;
- technical wiki administration;
- wiki management;

- community building;

- community support;

- promotion of the wiki;

- evaluation.

Depending on choices, wikis can be developed without programming or visual design skills, as these can be outsourced if you have the funds, or they might be found among the members of your wiki's community of readers and contributors. Content management skills need to be developed within the wiki community itself, and the wiki manager or another nominated person may need to use skills in social management for community building and community support if these do not come from within the community.

Deciding on use of categories and tags

If you expect the wiki to be moderately large, you may need a scheme for describing entries as an aid to browsing or searching. The two options most often used in wikis are categorisation and the use of tags (also known as labels).

With categorisation, a set of categories is used to classify wiki pages. Different wiki engines support different categorisation systems. In the simplest, a page is created for each category and a link is created from the category page to the wiki content page and vice versa. Because this approach relies on links, a page can be included in multiple categories. In most wikis, users are free to add new categories.

The use of tags in wikis is growing following the success of tagging in other social software. With tagging, users add their own tags or labels to each page. There is no pre-defined vocabulary. Tags are searchable. Some wiki engines provide maps of the tag space showing which tags are most popular (see Figure 7.2 for an example).

Assigning roles to users and setting access controls

Different wiki engines allow the setting of different access controls. These are based on roles. The main roles are reader, editor (contributor) and administrator. Depending on the wiki engine, you can set roles at the level of the wiki as a whole or for each page of the wiki. For example, you might decide to have a wiki open to all for reading and editing, but lock important pages so that they may only be edited by a wiki manager or users trusted with administrator access.

A key part of planning the wiki is determining who will be allowed to read and edit. Public wikis are open to all readers while private wikis restrict readership. Traditionally, wikis have been open to editing, but you may have reasons to limit editing to people who have a registered account. Making it harder to edit or to get an account increases the barrier to participation, making it more difficult to build up the wiki community, so you must balance how restricted you want access to be with how many people you want to attract to your community. If users feel empowered to make corrections, they can become part of the wiki rather than passive users of it.

Creating documentation and policies for the wiki

At some point, you will need rules for your wiki. These should be kept simple at first, and expanded when needed.

The complexity of rules is likely to grow with the wiki. Instructions may eventually get overly complex and detailed; this is known as 'instruction creep'.[3] It is important that newcomers are not put off by overly complex rules, though, and realise that they are welcome to add their content and have others apply the style rules to it later.

Wiki scope

Because of the ease of creating links to new pages, wikis can accumulate information that is outside the scope of the wiki. Several of Wikipedia's sister projects, such as Wiktionary (a dictionary) and Wikiquote (a collection of quotations), were started because visitors put non-encyclopaedic material into Wikipedia. Your mission statement should therefore make the limitations clear and lay down some core principles. In Wikipedia, one of the most frequently cited policies is called 'What Wikipedia is not', a page explaining what forms of content are not acceptable in Wikipedia.[4]

Ownership and intellectual property

Who owns a public wiki? Levels of ownership include the wiki site (e.g. a hosting service) and any trademarks or logos associated with the site and its name; the specific wiki and any trademarks or logos associated with the wiki; each page; and each edit of a page. At the wiki hosting service, Wikia, ownership is divided into the site and trademarks, which are owned by Wikia, Inc.; the copyright of a particular edit, which is owned by the person who made that edit; and ownership of the hosted wikis, which are owned by the wiki's community rather than by any one person.[5]

Intellectual property needs to be considered from two points of view: the copyright contained in material from other sources that contributors might want to add to your wiki, and ownership and management of the intellectual copyright of the material contained in your wiki.

It is important to document your policy on using material from other sources. Any item drawn from another source to be added to your wiki, including images, such as logos and photographs as well as text, is the intellectual property of its creator. You should have a policy of including only material that does not violate the copyright of the original creator. All sources should be acknowledged. When operating a public wiki, you need to have at least a basic idea of what is allowable under copyright law and what is not, or you may unwittingly become a host of infringing content.

When selecting the licence for your wiki, bear in mind whether your contributors will want to rely on material from another site. If so, you must pick either the same licence or a compatible licence. Some Creative Commons licences prevent modification of a work; these licences are not appropriate for wikis because the work is modified (a derivative version is created) each time a page is edited. Beware, too, of non-commercial-use only licences; they will limit the compatibility of your wiki with other sites, including all Wikimedia projects.

It is also important to decide on, and make clear to users and contributors, the policies associated with the intellectual property of material contained within your wiki. You may want to allow re-use of material in the wiki under a specific agreement such as the GNU Free Documentation License used by Wikipedia. If so, users will need to be advised that any material they include in the wiki can be re-used. You might want the intellectual property of all material in the wiki to be owned by the wiki community rather than the individual contributor; again, if this is the case, you need to advise contributors that assignment of copyright to the wiki community is a condition of contribution. You also need to make a clear written statement about conditions for re-use and acknowledgment of intellectual property. In public wikis, this statement usually appears on each page.

The intellectual property in collaboratively authored resources, such as wikis is a new area of law and some uncertainties are associated with it. Some guidance is provided by Creative Commons, which has produced a set of licences that might be applied in different situations.[6]

Making technical decisions

All of the issues considered during planning will help you to make a final decision about the wiki software to run. Identification of your resources and constraints will help you choose between the different wiki software paths available. The software will need to suit your purpose; for example, if it is important to convey a corporate identity, you will need a wiki that permits inclusion of your logo in the template; if you need to incorporate images or formulae, you will need a wiki engine that supports these formats. Identifying the potential users, both readers of and contributors to the wiki, is essential to understanding their requirements for the editing interface and other wiki features. Specifying security and access protocols and policies for the wiki will further narrow your wiki software decision. Chapter 7 gives more guidance on features and other technical issues.

Creating the wiki

Creating a wiki involves technical implementation, attention to visual design, establishing the initial content, testing the wiki, letting people know about the wiki, training, and motivating use and developing an initial community. The technical implementation is usually the simplest aspect of creating the wiki!

Technical implementation

The first step in creating a wiki is to activate it using the hosting service, appliance or software you have chosen. If you are using downloadable software, you will need to download it to your web server, install it and follow instructions for configuration. If you are using simple installation, this should be a quick and simple process.

Visual design

At an early stage, you will need to set up the template for displaying the wiki's content. Some wiki engines give little choice, while others prompt you to include a few elements, such as a logo and statement of intellectual property, and others permit extensive customisation of the visual design.

Several writers emphasise the predominance of content over visual appearance in wikis. Nonetheless, attention does need to be paid to the visual design in order to attract readers and contributors and, in many cases, to give the wiki a corporate or community image. This is not to say that the design needs to be elaborate, but it does recognise that visual design both establishes an emotional response and conveys information. Where possible, visual design should incorporate a logo that represents the company, group or community of the wiki. Visual design can also play an important role in navigation and in distinguishing one type of content from another. Consider the entries in Wikipedia: all entries have the same basic information structure, with each main section indicated by a new heading; almost every entry that is longer than one screen has a contents list near the top of the first screen. An early step in creating the wiki, then, is to identify which aspects of the visual design need to be established, to set up the template for the wiki, and if necessary, to document and prepare examples of pages with the preferred structure for individual entries.

Wiki content

Most wikis will need four types of content when they are initially created: a statement of purpose; information about the wiki founder(s) and contact details; documentation of policies and other rules or guidelines (including information about any categorisation scheme adopted); and help for new users. Many wikis will also need navigation guides, seed content, and perhaps a 'sandbox' where users can practise using the wiki. The amount of content, its nature, and the tone in which it is written will establish an initial sense of the wiki and the community that it supports.

Purpose

The purpose of the wiki should be clearly and briefly stated at the top of the front page. In many cases, it may also be useful to indicate the audience for the wiki immediately below the statement of purpose. Private or small group wikis might provide a list of or a link to a directory of group members, readers or contributors.

Information about the wiki and its founder(s)

Whether it is included on the front page, along with the purpose of the wiki, or as a separate 'about this wiki' page, it is useful for the users of most wikis to know something about the foundation of the wiki, such as the date of foundation, the names of the founders, their motivation for founding the wiki, and their contact details. In the case of a public wiki established or sponsored by an organisation, the 'about' page, should contain information about the organisation and links to key pages on the organisation's site.

Wiki documentation

The amount and type of documentation will depend on the nature of the wiki. A small wiki for use by a small, geographically collocated group for a short-term project may require little or no documentation. A larger, geographically distributed group is likely, however, to need some documentation. The policies established during planning will need to be recorded, usually on a separate wiki page. Intellectual property issues are so important to public wikis that they might warrant a separate page laying out both the need for contributors to respect the intellectual property of the creators of any works from which they draw material or inspiration, and the intellectual property policies for original content included in your wiki. A style guide or page template should be included for a wiki that will collect and provide information in the form of an encyclopaedia, dictionary, bibliography or other reference work. In a wiki that uses a categorisation scheme, the documentation will need to include a guide to the categorisation scheme and its use. A wiki that uses tags will also need information about tagging.

Even though it is simple to learn how to use a wiki, the administrators of wikis designed for more than a small group of users emphasise the importance of user guides. The user guide should describe how to use your specific wiki, rather than simply reiterate general information about how to use wikis. If a specific markup language is used, the details should be included in the user guide. The guide should also include, or link to, any policies or rules about use of the wiki. User guides often provide information about wikis in general, or a link to such information in another wiki. This is less important than the specific information about your wiki.

Wiki sandbox

A practice area, often called the 'sandbox' might encourage people to use the wiki. New users can be encouraged to use this area to practise their wiki skills before editing or contributing real content. On the other hand, you might prefer that new users are not distracted by a sandbox but discover the ease of using a wiki by editing live content.

Navigation guides

Organisation of the content will be important from the start. Because you are trying to attract users and encourage them to contribute to the project, the wiki needs to be easily usable. The homepage, or a sidebar, or both, should contain links to key information about the wiki and its use: user guides, style guides, categories, sandbox, about wiki. If this information is in the sidebar, the top link should, of course, be to the wiki front page. If the wiki is part of a larger site, there should be a link to the homepage of the parent site. You may also want to link to the homepages of any organisations that sponsor the wiki.

Seed content

Content creation begins with 'seed posting'. By building up some initial content, you can attract users and model the standards and style of the wiki from the beginning. Seed posts should include categories and tags if you want to encourage users to add them. If you do not have time to write a certain page yet, always make sure to at least leave a link to it, so others know that it should exist and will be encouraged to create it.

Testing the wiki

If possible, you should create the wiki in a private area, and test it before opening it to other users. Testing should involve proof-reading of all the initial content, and testing of all links, including any links from the template or sidebar. Technical tests should check that the edit, security, versioning, deletion and other basic functions of the wiki are all working. If any modifications have been made to the software, those modifications should be fully tested. If your wiki is going to represent your organisation in some way, we recommend that you also conduct at least some minimal usability testing with real users before launching the wiki.[7]

Letting people know about the wiki

When the basic structure of the wiki is ready, you may need to promote it to attract readers and contributors. You can advertise for new users on relevant mailing lists and through your own contacts. Explain to potential users that the wiki is a common effort so they feel they can get involved. Encourage people to visit the wiki and to become part of it. In the case of a private wiki, you will probably already have a list of members, but remember that you still need to launch the wiki and encourage visits and contributions.

You can publicise your wiki by adding it to the directories of wikis described in Chapter 3. Wiki Index, for example, lists both public and private wikis.

Training

If your wiki is used by a known group of users, you might consider the value of user training. A brief training session informs potential users about the wiki and its purpose, demonstrates how easy it is to use a wiki, and can be used to motivate users to add content from early in the life of the wiki. If not all potential users can be present at the training, training materials might be posted on the wiki. Successful training sessions can be conducted in one to two hours.

Initiating the wiki community

The success of a wiki depends on attracting contributors, the group often described as the 'wiki community'. Early contributors have the potential to form the nucleus of the community. These people may be especially enthusiastic about the topic and may even have past experience in similar communities. Inviting them to play specific roles in the wiki community (e.g. a personal invitation to add specific content, or to act as an administrator) can encourage their continued participation.

Sustaining growth and maintaining the wiki

As the wiki grows and its users take responsibility for it, some of the initial content will change and the nature of the wiki itself might change. As this occurs, you need to consider how to increase or maintain the number of users and build the user community, manage the content and deal with problem users and spam.

User community

Building a community of users will help to keep the wiki active beyond the initial stages. A strong community will encourage contributions and maintenance of the wiki and act as a source of skills for management of the wiki.

Good planning and attention to detail in creating the wiki help to attract contributors and build community. People are more inclined to contribute to wikis with a clear purpose that matches their own, which are clearly welcoming of contributors and which use devices, such as structure, style guides and simple help documentation to encourage tentative newcomers and socialise them to learn the formal and informal rules of the wiki.

Incentive systems can help to encourage participation. The rewards need not be tangible, but rather symbolic; for example, 'barn stars' are used in some wikis to reward contributors with a symbol of peer appreciation.[8] Caution should be taken over the type of contribution that is awarded, though. A system that encourages number of contributions over quality can be counterproductive. Wikipedia cautions against 'editcountitis', humorously described as 'a belief that a Wikipedian's overall contribution level can be measured solely by their edit count'.[9]

Wiki patterns are techniques that are known to work or not work in creating active wiki communities. A number of these patterns are documented at the Confluence site.[10] They include the champion pattern ('single wiki-nut, encourages coworkers to add, view, improve'), the trellis pattern ('egregiously boring content calls for fixing [e.g.,] *Wikitravel*: My city is more interesting than *that!*') and anti-patterns, such as the gate pattern ('too many procedural barriers to adding content').

The ways in which the wiki is being used should be evaluated regularly. Wikis need to be monitored for content quality, and also for activity to ensure areas are being updated. Nonetheless, a wiki manager should support and guide the community or team who are working on the wiki rather than micromanage them. Jonathan Huang, founder of the parody wiki encyclopaedia, Uncyclopedia, explains that over-management 'goes against the wiki spirit. In my conception, a wiki mustn't be micromanaged because it is defined by a culture of open-ness. The best strategy is to define a theme and let others fill this in.'[11]

Content management

Members of wiki communities use the recent changes feature of the wiki and feed aggregators to monitor changes to content. The recent changes feature allows members of the community to identify all changes in a given period. Feed aggregators alert those members of the community who are monitoring a specific page to changes on that page and, when no new feeds are detected, that the page has not been active. In large wikis, such as Wikipedia, volunteers monitor page changes, dealing with introduced errors, departures from policy, vandalism and spam. A volunteer responsible for a page will also update it if necessary. This system can be adapted for private wikis: responsibility for page monitoring can be assigned to a specific person who monitors page quality.

Most wikis will generate content that needs to be deleted. On public wikis, junk, spam, test edits, and vandalism, are obvious candidates for deletion, but even on private wikis, there will be a need to remove some content. Alternatives to deletion are merging pages together, or marking out-of-date pages as historic (and perhaps even hiding them from the wiki's search system).

A look at how the largest public wiki, the English Wikipedia, handles deletion can give some insight into how deletion can be handled in a public wiki. In January 2006, over 58,000 pages or images were deleted from the English Wikipedia. Deletion, which completely removes a page and its history from public view, can only be carried out by users with administrator access – something given to users who have earned the trust of the community over a few months of editing. The majority of deleted pages fall under Wikipedia's criteria for speedy deletion (spam, vandalism, test pages and so on) and are deleted by any administrator as soon as they are seen. Pages that might be deleted but which do not fall under the criteria for speedy deletion include non-verifiable information, content not suitable for an encyclopaedia, original research, advertising, and copyright infringements. This category of pages is listed for a period, often five days. During this period, the Wikipedia community can comment on whether a page ought to be deleted. Only where there is a rough consensus to delete the page will an administrator delete it. The deletion decision is sometimes questioned, and processes exist for the review of deleted pages.

Dealing with problem users

On a public wiki, an essential part of wiki management will be dealing with problem users. Potential problems arise from vandalism, trolling (the practice of adding material designed to anger readers or contributors), illegal content including copyright violations and libel, and the need to deal with users who cannot or will not abide by the community norms.

While many wiki engines include technical solutions for dealing with problem users, such as requiring registration or blocking a specific address or individual, the soft security approach (described in Chapter 1) is often preferred. Soft security relies on the wiki's users and norms to deal with problems. Many cases can be dealt with in this way. Often, it is sufficient to make the user aware of a copyright violation, or to roll back an instance of vandalism, for the user to recognise that the behaviour is not acceptable to the wiki community. On some occasions, though, the problem user persists with continued vandalism or plagiarism and the wiki manager needs to take specific action. Ward Cunningham describes how, while some users who initially try to vandalise WikiWikiWeb become part of the community, he has had to take action to limit the effect of one user who continued to vandalise the content. He noticed that the problem user made many more posts to the wiki in a day than other users, so his solution was to limit the daily number of posts any person could make.[12]

Building policies against copyright violations and requiring editors to cite their sources, especially for controversial content, can reduce the probability of legal problems on your wiki. Ideally, community norms will be strongly against illegal content and the community will act to remove any that is identified. A system of page monitoring helps with the process of checking content. Typically, a contributor or administrator will revert the damaged page to the previous version. If the problem page contains illegal content, it should be deleted.

Spam

Spam can be a problem for a public wiki. Increasingly, wiki engines are introducing techniques to detect and, in some cases, remove spam. A number of solutions are discussed on WikiWikiWeb.[13] Other solutions include reliance on members of the community to share page monitoring and revert those pages on which they notice spam; prevention of access to the wiki by any kind of bot (including search index bots); and user registration using the captcha system described in Chapter 7.

Evaluation

Both the wiki implementation project and the wiki itself should be evaluated. Wiki evaluation should be ongoing. As the lifecycle diagram in Figure 8.1 shows, evaluation can lead to revision of decisions made during initial planning, and to the wiki itself. A number of tools and methods are available to help evaluate wikis.

Evaluating the wiki implementation project

A wiki implementation project can be evaluated along all the dimensions used in planning the wiki:

- Is the wiki meeting its purpose? Has the nature of the wiki changed since it was launched and populated with content? Is any change congruent with your purpose? If not, is it worth pursuing a revised purpose? Should you take some other action?

- Has the wiki met its purpose, for example, to support a project, or should it be closed for some other reason? If so, plan for its closure, including removing the wiki from any directories and advising contributors of its closure.

- Is the wiki being used by its target audience? Have you attracted the contributors you want or has the wiki developed in the way you hoped?

- Are your access policies and security practices working effectively?

- Are the philosophy, policy and practices you established for the wiki being followed? If not, does it matter, and if it matters, what action will you take to get things back on track?

- Are you working within your financial, time, technology, and skill resources? Are more resources needed, and if so, how will you obtain them?

Evaluating the wiki

Throughout its life, the wiki should be evaluated, using not only the wiki project criteria, but criteria for evaluation of wikis in general. Among the questions to ask are:

- Does the content meet the quality standards established in Chapter 2? (See the questions for evaluation of wikis in Appendix B.)

- Does the structure support navigation?

- Can information in the wiki be found using the available navigation and finding tools?

- Are pages being maintained appropriately?

Wiki evaluation methods

Measurable indicators of success should be considered when planning the wiki so that it can later be evaluated against those measures. Three methods are available to help with wiki evaluation. Some wiki software produces statistics that can be used to monitor and evaluate a wiki, and server logs can be used to analyse traffic. You can also conduct user surveys to gauge the success of a wiki and to learn about changes that might be required.

Wiki statistics

A quantitative analysis of the wiki can be undertaken. Some wiki software will give automatic statistics on the number of users, edits and pages, and even show which pages have been edited or linked to most. The Wikistats package developed by Erik Zachte for MediaWiki can provide statistics on users (including the number of contributors, new users and active users), content (including total articles, new articles per day, edits per article, and article size, database size, number of words, number of internal and external links), and use (including visits per day and page requests per day).[14] Other statistics you may want to consider include: most edited pages, most linked to pages, and the average number of edits per user. Jakob Voss's statistical analysis of Wikipedia provides some indication of the type of analysis that can be produced.[15]

User surveys

User evaluation will involve going back to the wiki's mission statement and evaluating whether the target audience are reading or contributing to the wiki. A quality analysis can also be undertaken, through reader ratings or peer review of the content. Interview or questionnaire techniques can be useful in evaluating your wiki. Some typical questions you could ask the users of the wiki:

- Why do you use the wiki?
- How has it been valuable to you?

- Do you read or contribute to the wiki, or both?
- Which sections do you read/edit the most?
- Does anything prevent you from contributing to the wiki?

Notes

1. Andersen, E. (2005) 'Using wikis in a corporate context', in Hohenstein, A. and Wilbers, K. (eds) *Handbuch E-Learning*, Fachverlag Deutscher Wirtschaftsdienst; available at: *http://www.espen.com/papers/Andersen-2005-corpwikis.pdf* (accessed: 23 March 2006).

2. Some guidance is provided by Angeles, M. (2004) 'Using a wiki for documentation and collaborative authoring'; available at: *http://www.llrx.com/features/librarywikis.htm* (accessed: 6 September 2005); and Farkas, M. (2005) 'So you want to build a wiki?' *WebJunction*; available at:*http://webjunction.org/do/DisplayContent?id=11262* (accessed: 5 March 2006).

3. See the Wikimedia community's definition of *instruction creep* at: *http://meta.wikimedia.org/wiki/Instruction_creep* (page dated 18:51, 3 December 2005; accessed: 16 February 2006).

4. Wikipedia (2006) 'Wikipedia: what Wikipedia is not'; available at: *http://en.wikipedia.org/wiki/WP:NOT* (page dated 17:04, 13 March 2006; accessed: 14 March 2006).

5. Wikia (2005) 'Ownership'; available at: *http://www .wikia.com/wiki/Ownership* (page dated 00:28, 28 March 2006; accessed 13 April 2006).

6. See: *http://creativecommons.org./*

7. A wiki usability test is described in Desilets, A., Paquet, S. and Vinson, N.G. (2005) 'Are wikis usable?' *WikiSym '05, 16–18 October 2005, San Diego, CA.* National Research Council of Canada; available at: *http://www.wikisym.org/ws2005/ proceedings/paper-01.pdf* (accessed: 5 March 2006).

8. Meatball (2006) 'BarnStar'; available at: *http://www.usemod .com/cgi-bin/mb.pl?BarnStar* (page dated 07:59, 31 January 2006; accessed: 16 February 2006).

9. Wikipedia (2006) 'Editcountitis'; available at: *http:// en.wikipedia.org/wiki/Wikipedia:Editcountitis* (page dated 04:27, 21 February 2006; accessed: 26 February 2006).

10. See: *http://confluence.atlassian.com/display/PAT/Patterns+ of+Wiki+Adoption.*

11. Online communication in Wikicities IRC Channel, 19 February 2006.

12. Turnbull, G. (2004) 'Talking to Ward Cunningham about wiki', *Luvly*; available at: *http://gorjuss.com/luvly/20040406-wardcunningham.html* (accessed: 18 February 2006).

13. WikiWikiWeb (2006) 'Wiki spam'; available at: *http:// c2.com/cgi/wiki?WikiSpam* (page dated 20:12, 15 February 2006; accessed: 16 February 2006).

14. MediaWiki (2006) 'Wikistats'; available at: *http://meta .wikimedia.org/wiki/Wikistats* (page dated 22:44, 2 March 2006; accessed: 4 March 2006).

15. Voss, J. (2005) 'Measuring Wikipedia', *Proceedings of the 10th International Conference of the International Society for Scientometrics and Infometrics 2005, Stockholm, Sweden*; available at: *http://eprints.rclis.org/archive/00003610* (accessed: 21 April 2005).

9

Sources of information about wikis

This book has provided an introduction to wikis, their uses, their establishment and their management. Each of the chapters in this book includes references to additional sources of information about wikis and the thinking that underpins them. We have gathered some of the most important and most interesting for readers with a broad interest in wikis here, but remember to review the chapter resources if you are interested in a particular aspect of wikis.

Allison, P. (2005) 'High school students (and teachers) write collaboratively on a wiki', *Weblogs and Wikis and Feeds, Oh My! Paul Allison's Reflections on Teaching and Learning in New Territories*; available at: *http://www .nycwp.org/paulallison/2005/12/04* (accessed: 15 January 2006).

Andrus, D. C. (2005) 'The wiki and the blog: toward a complex adaptive intelligence community'; available at: *http://papers.ssrn.com/sol3/papers.cfm?abstract_id=7559 04* (accessed: 28 February 2006).

Angeles, M. (2004) 'Using a wiki for documentation and collaborative authoring'; available at: *http://www.llrx.com/ features/librarywikis.htm* (accessed: 6 September 2005).

Barton, M. (2004) 'Embrace the wiki way!' *Matt Barton's Tikiwiki*; available at: *http://mattbarton.net/tikiwiki/tiki-read_article.php?articleId=4* (accessed: 20 January 2006).

Bean, L. and Hott, D. D. (2005) 'Wiki: A speedy new tool to management projects', *Journal of Corporate Accounting and Finance* 16(5), 3–8.

Berners-Lee, T. (1999) 'Transcript of Tim Berners-Lee's talk to the LCS 35th Anniversary celebrations, Cambridge Massachusetts, 14 April 1999; available at: *http://www.w3.org/1999/04/13-tbl.html* (accessed: 18 February 2006).

Boyd, S. (2004) 'Wicked (good) wikis', *Darwin Magazine*, February; available at: *http://www.darwinmag.com/read/020104/boyd.html* (accessed: 27 February 2006).

Bridgewater, R. and Deitering, A.-M. (2005) 'Collaborating with wikis', paper presented at the Internet Librarian International 2005, London, 10–11 October 2005; available at: *http://www.vancouver.wsu.edu/fac/bridgewa/ili/* (accessed: 7 February 2006).

Ciffolilli, A. (2003) 'Phantom authority, self-selective recruitment and retention of members in virtual communities: The case of Wikipedia', *First Monday 8* (12); available at: *http://firstmonday.org/issues/issue8_12/ciffolilli* (accessed: 13 January 2006).

Clyde, L. A. (2005, April) 'Wikis', *Teacher Librarian* 32(4): 54–6.

Conlin, M. (2005) 'E-Mail is So Five Minutes Ago', *Business Week Online*; available at: *http://www.businessweek.com/magazine/content/05_48/b3961120.htm* (accessed: 23 December 2005).

Creative Commons. *Creative Commons Licenses*; available at: *http://creativecommons.org/licenses/* (accessed: 18 February 2006).

Delio, M. (2005) 'Enterprise collaboration with blogs and wikis', *Infoworld*; available at: *http://www.infoworld.com/article/05/03/25/13FEblogwiki_1.html* (accessed: 11 February 2005).

Dieberger, A. and Guzdial, M. (2003) 'CoWeb: Experiences with collaborative web spaces', In C. Lueg and D. Fisher (eds) *From Usenet to Cowebs: Interacting with Social Information Spaces*. London: Springer; pp. 155–66.

Ebersbach, A., Glaser, M. and Heigl, R. (2006) '*Wiki: Web Collaboration*. Berlin Heidelberg: Springer. [Originally published in German as *WikiTools*, Springer-Verlag, 2005, this book provides technical detail of establishing wikis using the MediaWiki and Twiki engines along with some general discussion of wiki structure and use.]

EDUCAUSE Learning Initiative (2005, corrected 17 February 2006) '7 Things you should know about wikis'; available at: *http://www.educause.edu/LibraryDetailPage/666?ID=ELI7004* (accessed: 18 February 2006).

Fernando, A. (2005) 'Wiki: the new way to collaborate', *Communication World*, 22(3), 8–19.

Gilbane Report (2005) 'Survey on enterprise, blog and wiki use', *Gilbane Report*; available at: *http://gilbane.com/surveys.html* (accessed: 11 February 2006).

Giles, J. (2005) 'Internet encyclopaedias go head to head', *Nature* 438, 900–1; available at: *http://www.nature.com/nature/journal/v438/n7070/pdf/438900a.pdf* (accessed: 18 February 2006).

Glaser, M. (2004). 'Collaborative conundrum: Do wikis have a place in the newsroom?' *Online Journalism Review*; available at: *http://ojr.org/ojr/glaser/1094678265.php* (accessed: 18 February 2006).

Goodnoe, E. (2005) 'How to use wikis for business', *InformationWeek*; 8 August; available at: *http://informationweek.com/story/showArticle.jhtml?articleID=167600331* (accessed: 17 September 2005).

James, H. (2004). 'My brilliant failure: Wikis in classrooms' *Kairosnews*, 21 May 2004; available at: *http://kairosnews .org/node/3794* (accessed: 18 February 2006).

Lamb, B. (2004) 'Wide open spaces: Wikis, ready or not', *EDUCAUSE Review* 39(5); available at: *http://www .educause.edu/ir/library/pdf/erm0452.pdf* and *http:// www.educause.edu/pub/er/erm04/erm0452.asp* (accessed: 18 February 2006).

Leuf, B. and Cunningham, W. (2001) *The Wiki Way: Quick Collaboration on the Web.* Boston: Addison-Wesley. [This is primarily a technical book, much loved by wiki developers and administrators. It also contains observations on the nature of wikis and wiki management.]

Mattison, D. (2003) 'Quickiwiki, Swiki, Twiki, Zwiki and the plone wars: Wiki as a PIM and collaborative content tool', *Searcher* 11(4); available at: *http://www.infotoday .com/searcher/apr03/mattison.shtml* (accessed: 5 January 2006).

Mattison, D. (2005) 'Blog and wiki technology collaborative document: new outline-style version of blogs-RSS-Atom-wikis collaborative document'; available at: *http://www .davidmattison.ca/tiki/tiki-index.php?page_ref_id=12* (page dated 03:00, 4 December; accessed: 9 January 2006).

McKiernan, G. (2005) 'Wiki bibliography'; available at: *http://www.public.iastate.edu/~CYBERSTACKS/WikiBib .htm* (accessed: 18 February 2006).

Roberts, A. (2005) 'Introducing a WIKI to a community of practice'; available at: *http://www.frankieroberto.com/ dad/ultrastudents/andyroberts/year2/AEreport/AEtool.ht ml* (accessed: 9 January 2006).

Schwartz, L., Clark, S., Cossarin, M. and Rudolph, J. (2004) 'Educational wikis: Features and selection criteria', *International Review of Research in Open and Distance*

Learning 5(1); available at: *http://www.irrodl.org/ content/v5.1/technote_xxvii.html* (accessed: 18 February 2006).

Skiba, D. J. (2005) 'Do your students wiki?', *Nursing Education Perspectives* 26(2): 120–1.

Stenmark, D. (2005) 'Knowledge sharing on a corporate intranet: effects of re-instating web authoring capability', *Proceedings of ECIS 2005, Regensburg, Germany, 26–8 May 2005*; available at: *http://www.informatik.gu.se/ ~dixi/publ/ecis_27.pdf* (accessed: 14 January 2006).

Surowiecki, J. (2004) *The Wisdom of Crowds*. New York: Doubleday.

Terdiman D. (2005) 'How wikis are changing our view of the world', *CNET News.com*; available at: *http://news .com.com/Wikis+allow+news,+history+by+committee/20 09-1025_3-5944453.html* (accessed: 18 February 2006).

Venners, B. (2003) 'Exploring with wiki: a conversation with Ward Cunningham', *Artima Developer*; available at: *http://www.artima.com/intv/wiki.html* (accessed: 11 February 2006).

Wagner, C. (2004) 'Wiki: A technology for conversational knowledge management and group collaboration', *Communications of the Association for Information Systems* 13, 265–89; available at: *http://cais.isworld .org/articles/1319/default.asp?View=Journal&x=31&y=13* (accessed: 27 February 2006).

Wenger, E. (1998) *Communities of Practice: Learning, Meaning, and Identity*. Cambridge, UK: Cambridge University Press.

Wood, L. (2005) 'Blogs and wikis: technologies for enterprise applications?', *The Gilbane Report* 12(10); available at: *http://www.gilbane.com/gilbane_report.pl/ 104/* (accessed: 18 February 2006).

Blogs about wikis

Two regularly updated blogs about wikis are:

Mayfield, R. *Social Software Blog*; available at: *http://www
.socialtext.com/*. (Ross Mayfield is the founder of
Socialtext, Inc. and blogs on the corporate website.)

Portante, T. *Wikisquared*; available at: *http://www
.wikisquared.com/*.

Two educational technology bloggers also talk about wikis:

Allison, P. *Weblogs and Wikis and Feeds, Oh My!*; available
at: *http://www.nycwp.org/paulallison/*.

Richardson, W. *Weblogg-ed*; available at: *http://www
.weblogg-ed.com/*.

Appendix A:
Comparison of wiki sites with websites

Websites	Wiki sites
Information provision philosophy	Collaborative, exploratory philosophy
Content displayed in a browser on Internet or intranet	Same
Editing often requires HTML	Simple editing with simple markup or WYSIWYG
New page is created as a new file before it can be linked to existing pages	New pages added by creating a link within an existing page
Pages become 'live' at a time decided by the administrator	Pages are updated in real time unless content approval is activated
Each page has few authors	Each page can have many authors
Authors are known	Authors may be anonymous
Editing is limited to authorised persons	Editing may be open to all readers without registration
Versioning system must be developed to keep old versions	Old versions of pages are usually kept automatically
May not be possible to restore an earlier version	Usually possible to restore earlier version of a page
Reversion requires some effort	Reversion is quick and simple, requiring one or two clicks
No recent changes facility	Recent changes to pages can be tracked
Users can be alerted to changes in pages	Same

Websites	Wiki sites
Accessible pages are searchable using standard Web search engines	Same
Search can be quite sophisticated	Most wikis offer rudimentary search within the wiki
Hierarchical permissions structure	Simple permissions structure
Content approval processes are common	Content approval processes are rarely implemented
Content defined by author or sponsor of page	Content defined by community of authors
Site structure is pre-defined	Structure of wiki develops as pages are added by users
May support an existing community, but not a community development tool	Possibility of developing a community of readers and contributors
Pages considered finished	Pages considered always in process

This is a revision and extension of a model first proposed by Arreguin, C. (2004) 'Wikis', in B. Hoffman (ed.) *Encyclopedia of Educational Technology*; available at: *http://coe.sdsu.edu/eet/articles/wikis/start.htm* (accessed: 6 September 2005)

Appendix B:
Questions for evaluation of wikis as sources of information

Criteria for assessing information content

Purpose

- What is the aim or purpose of the wiki? Who are the intended readers (and contributors)?
- Is that aim or purpose aligned to the needs of users?
- To what extent is the aim or purpose achieved through the wiki?

Scope and coverage

- Is the intended scope and coverage made clear?
- Is the scope and coverage aligned to the aim or purpose of the wiki?
- Is the scope and coverage aligned to the needs of users?
- How comprehensive is the coverage of the topic? Are there any gaps in coverage?

- How deep is the coverage of the topic? Is there coverage more deep in some areas than others?
- Are there references to other sources of information on the topic? What is the quality of those sources?

Authority

- What organisation (if any) is behind the wiki as sponsor or publisher?
- Does the wiki provide information about the sponsor or publisher?
- Who is responsible for the information content?
- Is there some form of peer review or editorial control?
- What is known of the qualifications, expertise or reputation in their field of contributors and any reviewers or editors?
- Is the wiki listed by reliable directories or reference sites?
- Is it possible to track changes to the wiki? Is there any limitation to the time period or number of changes that can be tracked?
- What mechanism is there for identifying the person who contributed each change? Is it possible to make anonymous contributions or contributions under a pseudonym?
- Do contributors need to register? How extensive is the information required for registration?

Accuracy

- How accurate is the information?
- Can the information be verified through other sources?

- Does the content reflect a particular point of view? Is there any evidence of bias?

- Is the information presented in a way that inspires confidence? Are there any spelling errors or grammatical errors? What is the quality of the writing?

- Are sources of content documented and referenced?

Currency

- Does the wiki include information that enables currency to be evaluated?

- Is the textual information current?

- Are photographs and other visual features current?

- Does each wiki page include information about the date and time of the last update?

Criteria for assessing features of online resources

Format

- How appropriate is the format of the wiki, bearing in mind the aim or purpose and the intended audience?

- How appropriate is the format of the wiki, bearing in mind the subject?

- Is the structure of the wiki clear? Is it well organised?

Appearance

- How attractive is the front page? What impression does it give to the reader?

- Is the appearance aligned with the aim or purpose, the content and the intended audience?

- Is colour used appropriately for font face, links, background?

- Is the size of the font appropriate given the aim or purpose and the intended users?

- Are images included? If so, are they well laid out on the page?

Navigation

- Is the wiki easy to navigate?

- Are navigation features consistent throughout the wiki?

- How easy is it to find an item of information that should be on the wiki?

- Is there an up-to-date site map or some indication of how the wiki is structured?

- Can users search the wiki? If so, how well does the search engine work? How easy is it to use? How easy is it to interpret and follow the results of a search?

Links

- Are the links relevant and appropriate given the aim or purpose and the intended users?

- Are the links working?

- Are the links the best available on the topic?

- Are the links described in an appropriate way?

- Is it easy for readers to distinguish external links from the content of the wiki itself and from links to other pages within the particular wiki?

User needs

- In what language or languages is the wiki available?

- Can the wiki be used by people with vision problems? Does the wiki work with assistive technology, such as screen readers for the blind?

- Can the wiki be used by people with impaired hearing?

- Is there any evidence of usability testing of the wiki?

- Is the information contained in the wiki publicly available for all users? Is access to all or some of the content restricted by password? Is payment required for access to some parts?

Technical aspects

- Does the wiki work well in any browser? Is a specific version of a browser required?

- Does the wiki load quickly?

- Is the wiki available most of the time, or are there periods when it is down?

- Do users need to scroll through long pages?

- How well do the pages print out? If the page structure is complex, is a 'print format' available?

Criteria specific to evaluation of wikis

Reliability

- How often is the wiki changed?

- Is the frequency of changes appropriate to the purpose, scope and audience of the wiki?

- To what extent does the informational content change with updates?

- Do the changes improve the content?

- Is there evidence of edit wars?

- Does the wiki community have a mechanism for resolving content disputes?

- Is there evidence of effective strategies for dealing with spam and vandalism?

Features

- How well does the wiki use the standard features of wiki software?

- Is there a mechanism for annotating changes, e.g. summarising the content of a change or noting that the change is minor? Is that mechanism used by the contributors?

- Does the wiki enable discussion of the content of each page, separately from the page itself?

- Is there an RSS or Atom feed? How easy is it to find information about how to set up the feed?

Index

Printed in the United States
78389LV00001B/113